Indiana Artists George Jo and Evelynne Bernloehr Mess

Indiana Artists George Jo and Evelynne Bernloehr

MESS

A Story of Devotion by June DuBois
with "A History of Printmaking in Indiana" by Martin F. Krause

© 1985 Indiana Historical Society

Library of Congress Cataloging in Publication Data

DuBois, June, 1927-
    Indiana artists George Jo and Evelynne Bernloehr Mess.

    Includes bibliographies and index.
    1. Mess, George Joseph, 1989-1962. 2. Daily,
Evelynne Mess, 1903-   .   3. Artists—Indiana—
Biography. 4. Prints—Indiana. I. Krause, Martin F.
History of printmaking in Indiana. 1985. II. Indiana
Historical Society. III. Title.
N6537.m48D8   1985   760'.092'2 [B]   85-7596
ISBN 0-87195-000-6

Contents

Illustrations

Evelynne Mess, *Adirondack Trail*, 1945, aquatint

Preface

Indiana artists Evelynne Bernloehr Mess (now Evelynne Mess Daily) and George Jo Mess have endowed Indiana and indeed the nation with a legacy to be cherished. Like the works of their fellow regionalists Thomas Hart Benton and Grant Wood, the Messes' thoughtfully executed prints and genre paintings deepen our knowledge of the recent past and fill us with a nostalgia for the simpler times before World War II.

Especially as printmakers—in George's case, as a maker of aquatint etchings, and in Evelynne's, as a worker in all print media—these artists made lasting contributions to Indiana art.

Their careers as artists-in-partnership are described in the pages that follow. This study was prompted by Evelynne, who suggested that I "write a biography of George Jo Mess." While it is typical of her self-effacing approach that she conceived of the project as a biography of her husband,

in fact they were partners in art as well as in the rest of their life together, and any biography of either would need to be a biography of both. I have attempted in this narrative to disclose their individuality as artists and persons, but their lives also offer many insights into the challenges and rewards of marriages that also operate as creative partnerships.

I would like to thank the Indiana Historical Society for making this book possible. Thanks, too, to Robert Yassin, director of the Indianapolis Museum of Art, for his timely advice and to the Indianapolis poet and novelist Vesle Fenstermaker for her helpful suggestions.

Thanks also to Wilbur Meese and the late Floyd Hopper for generous telephone interviews and to Lana Ruegamer of the Indiana Historical Society for assistance with research and editorial advice, to Gayle Thornbrough for her care and advice, to Kent Calder for his final editing, and to Martin F. Krause, associate curator of prints and drawings, Indianapolis Museum of Art, for the accompanying essay.

But the greatest tribute in preparing this work must go to Evelynne Mess Daily, whose idea it was and whose meticulous care in keeping records has been an invaluable aid to research. Even more important have been her unfailing helpfulness, good spirits, and patient cooperation in the search for the most accurate possible presentation.

June DuBois

Evelynne Charlien Bernloehr, ca. 1904

Chapter 1

Evelynne Bernloehr
childhood and youth

Tʜᴇʀᴇ ᴡᴇʀᴇ ᴏɴ Nᴏʀᴛʜ Aʟᴀʙᴀᴍᴀ Sᴛʀᴇᴇᴛ in 1903 some of the most elegant residences in the then relatively young city of Indianapolis. Proud, solid, neat, with well-kept lawns and gardens, the houses marched up the tree-lined brick street, which for added tone boasted a green and flower-bedded "boulevard" in the center, running all the way from the mile square to Twenty-second Street.

Alabama Street represented and contained in microcosm the results of the material and a certain aesthetic, if not spiritual, satisfaction shared by many Americans of the times. The middle-class Hoosiers who dwelt here had sprung from European backgrounds, predominantly Scots-Irish and German. Dedication to the puritan ethic directed their lives. They loved their country and its freedoms with a passion. They believed in the American Dream.

And why shouldn't they? Why, a man who was willing to work hard and sacrifice a bit for almost any career he might choose during his early years had strong prospects of owning a fine house on Alabama Street long before he reached middle age and, furthermore, of filling it with a devoted family of which he could be proud.

And what about a woman? Were a variety of careers open to her, too? We all know the answer to that. Although American women had been attending colleges and universities in increasing numbers since the 1870s and had pioneered in professions and the arts before 1900, most women were still expected to devote their lives to husbands and families. Generally speaking, if a woman chose not to become attached to a promising young man—or to any man, for that matter—she might spend her life as a teacher or a nurse. Those pur-

suits would be open to her providing she had been able to afford education enough to follow them. The uneducated faced dreary and low-paying jobs in factories, stores, offices, and domestic service, or continued to slave on the farms just as they always had, married or not.

It is perhaps charitable to suggest that successful men on the Alabama streets of those days naively supposed their wives and daughters preferred a "protected" life of virtual servitude. And even in those rare instances where a father recognized and encouraged talent in his daughter by sending her to college or an academy to perfect her skills in music or painting or writing, she was likely to have been so completely brainwashed by the society in which she lived that she would have had little faith in herself.

Only a woman driven by some inexplicable inner force could transcend such limitations. Such was the case of Evelyn (later Evelynne) Charlien Bernloehr, whose life represents both the accomplishments and constraints of American women artists of her generation.

Evelynne lived on North Alabama Street in Indianapolis from January 8, 1903, the date of her birth, until April 28, 1925, the date of her marriage. She was one of six children (three boys and three girls) born to John A. (1874-1933) and Anna Giezendanner (1871-1956) Bernloehr.[1] John Bernloehr's parents had emigrated from Germany to Indianapolis in the 1860s, and in 1849 the Giezendanners had found their way from Switzerland to the Indiana capital and established a wholesale bakery in downtown Indianapolis. Both families had brought with them skills, knowledge, and tastes in fine arts and music.

John Bernloehr expressed his appreciation for art in a number of ways. As an importer of fine jewelry, he made a good living for his family in the jewelry shop (Chris Bernloehr Bros.) he owned in partnership with his brother, located in an arcade at Virginia Avenue and Washington Street. In building and furnishing their house, John and Anna Bernloehr revealed an imaginative discrimination in their selection of appurtenances such as leaded glass windows, Tiffany stained glass lamps, and other fixtures in etched glass imported from Europe. On the walls hung oil paintings, some painted in Indiana, others in Germany and Switzerland. The large doorways between rooms in the main living area were decorated with panels of wood carvings.

Evelynne recalls tea tables laden with refreshments, which included pastries from Giezendanner Swiss bakery. Such tables were decorated with Anna Bernloehr's hand-embroidered linen, gleaming silver, and delicate Bavarian china, all to be revealed to guests following an evening of music or recitations.

"Our house was filled with music all the time," Evelynne says,

> Both of my parents were musicians. My father directed an orchestra made up mostly of stringed instruments. They played all kinds of entertainments around the city the whole time I was growing up. They were always playing in our music room. It was wonderful. I used to like to listen to them as I stretched out on a bench along the walls of our stair landing, especially at night when I could watch the stars twinkling through the tall, tall window that reached all the way up to the ceiling of the second floor. And when they played for parties in the ballroom on the third floor—well, I just loved it all. I had a wonderful happy life with my family.
>
> And we had many friends, too. My parents were active in all sorts of community affairs. And you can imagine how often our house was literally filled with youngsters when I tell you that we four children were really extroverts when it came to making friends. But as a family, we were also sufficient unto ourselves, you might say. We kids did everything together—amateur theatricals, musical programs, sports, why we even went down to the

Athenaeum in a group to participate in a calisthenics class every week. And we did our share, too, in community affairs. My sister and I worked several summers to raise money for the fresh-air fund.

Proficiency in music became one of Evelynne's goals during her childhood. Encouraged by her parents, she studied the piano at the Metropolitan School of Music (which later merged with the Jordan College of Fine Arts) and the Indianapolis College of Musical Art, then located in the 800 block on North Pennsylvania Street. It was also during her preteen years that her father taught her to play the mandolin, guitar, and banjo. Appreciation of good music, both as a participant and responsive listener, remained for her an important avocation in a life filled with artistic interests and pursuits.

An interest in writing developed in her early teens, at which time she wrote a number of short stories. One, entitled "A Southern Story," she bound and illustrated and dedicated with the following poem:

> I turn to you, dear Mother, and give
> Into your hand my little book,
> Since through the years and while I live
> It is to you I still must look
> For hand of strength, for heart of cheer,
> For all that's wise and kind and dear.

However, the love of the life of Evelynne Bernloehr has not been music or poetry but, rather, drawing, drawing, drawing and all manner of art related to it. "I was always drawing, even as a little girl in a high chair," she recalls. "I guess I stayed in a high chair longer than most children because I was never very big"—as a grown woman she never quite reached a height of five feet—

> but I remember sitting there for long periods perfectly content with pencil and paper, drawing everything I could see or think of. As I look back on those times, I think my mother must have been grateful for the serenity thus provided. She loved gardening, for one thing, and my happy occupation with pencil and paper provided the chance to indulge in that hobby a bit. Our house was filled with flowers. I drew and painted them whenever I could.

Evelynne Mess, *Street Musicians*, 1929, etching

Fortunately, the Bernloehrs recognized their children's gifts. (An older sister of Evelynne's, Lenora Bernloehr Daily, excelled as a fashion artist.) As a child, Evelynne was given a "studio," a small room adjacent to the large bedroom she shared with her sister. Responding to his daughter's preoccupation with drawing, John Bernloehr gave Evelynne her first professional quality paints when she was only seven years old. Though she made friends easily among children at her neighborhood school, School No. 45, Evelynne spent most of her after-school hours and weekends at her drawing table instead of playing dolls with her friends. Her father's jewelry business also fascinated her, and she often attempted to capture the glitter of precious stones in her drawing and painting. Many years later, when she took courses in jewelry-making, a taste for fashioning fine pieces seemed to come to her naturally.

In those pre-World War I days, correspondence schools in art flourished. Some of their advertising consisted of offering prizes to aspiring young artists for drawing, painting, and sculpting. Although the aim was to enroll new students and the prizes were modest, the advantages for participants were obvious. And what a thrill it was when that first-prize five-dollar check came in the mail! Even the letter in which the young artist received praise from so august an institution provided great satisfaction. Evelynne tasted that kind of sweet success as far back as her grade school days, during which she also won prizes in local poster contests sponsored by schools and small business firms.

Indianapolis was not a bad place for an artistic child to grow up in during the early decades of the twentieth century. Although the city lacked a major art collection, there resided within the Hoosier capital a dedicated group of persons committed to building an institution to make art available to the public. The Art Association of Indianapolis was founded in 1883 by the extraordinary May Wright Sewall, an Indianapolis educator and feminist with a national reputation as a reformer and clubwoman in the pre-World War I period. The association organized exhibits and various art schools, operating on a very limited budget, until John Herron, a

local businessman, left them over $200,000 in 1895. By 1906 the association had erected the John Herron Art Institute at Sixteenth and Pennsylvania streets, and the associated art school was established.[2]

But for the artistic Indianapolis child an equally important influence was probably Wilhelmina Seegmiller, director of art instruction in the Indianapolis Public Schools from 1893 until her sudden death in 1913 at the age of forty-six.[3] An exceptional administrator and teacher, Seegmiller was largely responsible for resources of the Herron Institute and its art school being made available to public school pupils. Prompted by her, the Art Association secured legislation from the Indiana General Assembly in 1909 requiring the local school commissioners to underwrite the greater use of the museum and art school by schoolchildren, and through one of the provisions at least fifty public school students a year were to be awarded scholarships to the art school.[4]

When Evelynne was twelve years old, she won the first of six annual scholarships to the John Herron Art School. The classes, in which drawing and lettering were the main subjects taught, convened every Saturday morning during the school year. These she attended as a scholarship student through the seventh and eighth grades and during her four years at Arsenal Technical High School.

The Bernloehrs spent summers in their cottage on Lake James, a small resort community in northern Indiana, not far from Fort Wayne. The bucolic atmosphere created limitless opportunities for the children to explore the countryside with and without their parents. Evelynne recalls happy times of shared nature walks with her mother:

I was interested in everything we saw—flowers, trees, weeds, frogs, butterflies, fish, turtles, rocks, snakes. And I always had some kind of collection going. Yes, even snakes, though that was a mistake, because the eggs I had thought were turtle eggs hatched out some garter snakes, which didn't prove entirely popular with the rest of the family. But I know those long summer days when I was so free to roam, especially as a child, definitely influenced

Evelynne Mess, *Porte de Samois*, 1929, etching

me in the subject matter I still choose to draw and paint and etch.

When I was twelve and thirteen, I also got acquainted with Brown County when my family sent me to Hill Top Camp during those summers. Short periods, you know, because of course I couldn't bear the thought of not going to Lake James with the family. But I loved camp life down there in those beautiful hills.

Little did she dream, in those days, of the lasting role nature and Brown County would play in her life and work. Practically all of her mature works as an etcher are nature studies. Even those which are not still reveal an artist whose affections lie close to nature and the outdoors.

Etching fascinated Evelynne from childhood. She was attracted to drawings in the Indianapolis *Star* signed by Frederick Polley, who taught art at the Arsenal Technical High School. But when she enrolled in his class, she found to her disappointment that he did not teach etching, nor was etching taught in the prestigious Shortridge High School, where she took a year of post-graduate art work in 1920-21.

Evelynne Mess, from a potrait by Robert Long

Knowing that etching courses were not available at the John Herron school, Evelynne attempted to obtain her parents' permission to study at the Art Institute of Chicago. Protective of their daughter, they refused to send her so far away from home, however much they approved her ambition. Instead, they persuaded her to enroll in Butler University in the fall of 1921 to prepare for a career of teaching art.

However, after one year of study Evelynne chose to leave the university, though some courses she had taken there would later make it possible for her to meet the requirements for a teaching certificate. The autumn of 1922 found her back at the John Herron school, this time as a full-time student, studying painting with the highly regarded artists William Forsyth and Clifton Wheeler. There she remained for two years, at one point practice teaching in the Saturday morning classes to complete the work required for a teaching certificate in art. She also availed herself of academic courses brought to the Herron school from Indiana University.

There were still no etching courses listed in the Herron catalogue. Fearing that her chances of learning the art were probably going to remain nonexistent indefinitely in local schools, the young woman set forth to teach herself. The public library, she decided, would be the right place to start. Surely among all those hundreds of books there must be a recipe for making etchings.

And indeed there was. For a starter, she found a thorough discussion—a history of the subject and those who developed the art—in the eleventh edition of the *Encyclopedia Britannica*. And fortunately Evelynne was not alone in her interest in etching. In January, 1924, twenty students formed a print class to hear lectures on appreciating engraving and etching. Evelynne's former teacher Polley performed a demonstration lecture, explaining the rudiments of etching. Later in 1924 during her second and last year as a student at Herron, Evelynne was assisted by the timely publication of the book which eventually became her bible on etching, *The Art of Etching*, by E. S. Lumsden (New York: Dover, 1924).

Evelynne Mess, *Old Montmarte*, 1929, etching

Evelynne Mess, *Backyard in Episy*, 1929, etching

By this time Evelynne had become familiar with certain tools that she needed for etching, but they were at that time unavailable in Indianapolis. A dentist neighbor, impressed by her dedication, fashioned some of his old instruments into etching needles and gave them to her. Although her first etching plate was made of zinc rather than copper, it provided a suitable surface for experimenting with the new needles. But a major obstacle was the fact that she had no press; thus the question of where she would find high-quality rag paper was only academic. (Later she would send to London, Paris, and Tokyo for the needed material until she found an importing firm in New York through which she could order it.)

In the fall of 1924 the would-be etcher was offered the position of art teacher at Manual Training High School. The tradition of art instruction at Manual was an honorable one. But, though she accepted the job, she did not really relish the role of teacher. Part of the problem lay in what a famous St. Louis cook once said about *her* job: "It's so daily." An early riser and indefatigably industrious, Evelynne objected to teaching not from lethargy but from her impatience to get on with her own creative work. Teaching robbed her of the large blocks of time she wanted to spend on her own projects. Besides, she feared that the teaching routine would remove her from the art pulse of the community.

She stayed with the job throughout the school year and did the only thing she knew how to do, that is, to give her best to the work and the students. Only twenty-one years old and very small, as has been noted, she found herself teaching perspective to senior boys who towered over her. It was a strong testimony to her poise and gifts that she carried off this role with success. However, though appreciative of the school board's wish to renew her contract the following year, she declined the offer.

In the meantime, determined to keep in touch with life in the art world of the city, she worked as an assistant to the director of the Herron Art School in night classes. During that period she met a young man, one of the students enrolled in a

drawing class taught by the Indianapolis artist William Forsyth. His name was George Mess.

Notes

1. Two of the Bernloehr children died in childhood. Among the four who lived to adulthood were Evelynne, Lenora (1900-1980), Wilmer (1898-1963), and John (b. 1913), an optometrist who resides in Battle Creek, Michigan.

2. May Wright Sewall, "The Art Association of Indianapolis, Indiana: A Retrospect," in *Art Association of Indianapolis, Indiana, A Record, 1883-1906* (Indianapolis: Hollenbeck Press, 1906), pp. 5-28. For Sewall, see sketch in *Notable American Women*.

3. See chapter on Seegmiller in Mary Q. Burnet, *Art and Artists of Indiana* (New York: Century Co., 1921; reprinted Evansville, Ind.: Unigraphics, 1981), pp. 257-67.

4. Indianapolis Public Schools, *Annual Report*, 1908-1909, pp. 94-95; Burnet, *Art and Artists of Indiana*, p. 264.

George Joseph Mess, ca. 1899

Chapter 2

George Mess
childhood and youth

Your little sketch found favor in the eyes of the judges, and we are presenting you with our check for $1.00, one of the 150 - $1.00 prizes. You may know that you have shown quite a bit of talent as there were some 20,000 sketches in the School-child's Contest alone.

Please remember the little NATIONAL OATS Girl and tell all your friends about her. We are going to give another contest soon and hope you will take part again.

Don't forget that the little NATIONAL OATS Girl is your friend.[1]

Typical of messages received by George Mess during his childhood and youth, the above letter was written by the advertising manager of the National Oats Company of St. Louis. In those days, contests to encourage children's artistic endeavors were common occurrences, sponsored by industries throughout the nation. Undoubtedly, such advertising schemes proved profitable for the companies. But those young artists who entered the contests obviously profited too. Many, like George Mess, simply enjoyed expressing themselves with pencil and brush. Like other dedicated artists in all fields, George could not recall a time when he was not drawing or painting or when he believed he would ever be anything but an artist.

Among his most treasured childhood prizes was a complete leatherbound set of Shakespeare, awarded by a local Indianapolis business, Stewart's Book Company, for his design of a bookplate. But perhaps even more important than his frequent triumphs in art contests was the encouragement he received at home. His father, Joseph Mess, an artistic, sensitive man, understood his son's creative nature and need to express himself. George's birthday and Christmas presents from him always included a sketchbook and other art materials.

George Joseph Mess was born in Cincinnati on June 30, 1898, the second son of photoengraver Joseph J. Mess (1871-1933) and his wife Anna Gleis Mess (1875-1960). Both parents were native-born Cincinnatians. Joseph's parents were born in Germany; Anna's mother was German-born, her father Dutch.[2] And both parents had known tragedy in early life. Joseph's father was killed by a runaway horse and wagon when Joseph was only twelve years old. As the oldest child, Joseph Mess helped his mother support his younger brothers and sister by shining shoes. Anna Gleis's mother died when Anna was five years old, and the little girl was reared by a stepmother. But although their backgrounds were similar, George Mess's parents did not have similar temperaments. In this family the father was the gentle figure, while the mother was the stern disciplinarian. Joseph and Anna Mess had three sons, Arthur, George, and Gordon. Unsurprisingly, the boys took their artistic father as their model, and all became artists of one sort or another.

Anna's insistence on discipline may have impressed her family as overly burdensome, perhaps even cold, but what a responsibility for her! The formation of the characters of three artists had been thrust into her hands. All well and good, she thought, were gentleness, tenderness, sensibility, imagination, empathy, and all those other qualities supposedly shared by artists. But what is an artist without discipline? And what better place to develop that necessary virtue than at home?

In November, 1899, when George Mess was still a baby, his parents left Cincinnati and moved to Indianapolis. The impetus for his parents' move was the opportunity for Joseph Mess to manage the photoengraving department of the Indianapolis *News*, a major daily newspaper. As foreman of this department of skilled craftsmen, Joseph Mess made a comfortable living for the next thirty-three years, providing a pleasant home for his family in increasingly prosperous neighborhoods. Until 1911 the Mess family lived at 2437 East Michigan Street; from 1911 until 1920—throughout George Mess's high school years and beyond—the family lived at 3117 Park Avenue, a comfortable middle-class neighborhood near Fall Creek.

George Mess and his brothers spent most of their grammar school years at School 15 (later called the Thomas Gregg School) at Belville Avenue and East Michigan, just around the corner from their house. Photographs of George Mess as a schoolboy show a large, happy, healthy-looking child, but despite his appearance of radiant health the youngster suffered a severe illness. When he was seven George contracted pneumonia and typhoid fever and had to spend "one year in bed" and then learn to walk all over again. Presumably that "year" in bed was one in which the boy entertained himself through the long hours, days, and weeks by drawing and painting. Pencil and paper, crayons and paints provided an almost constant source of diversion. What was solace to the seven-year-old grew to be a lifelong preoccupation.

By the time he was ten years old George's artistic gifts had already attracted attention. Along with his older brother Arthur he was painting in oils. George and Arthur each copied a well-known painting to raise money for the local "fresh-air fund" (donations solicited by newspapers in the early decades of the century to send city children to rural campsites in the summertime). Their work was successful enough to be exhibited publicly and to be featured in the Indianapolis *News*.

After George transferred to the William Bell School, No. 60, at Thirty-third and North Pennsylvania in consequence of his parents' move to Park Avenue in 1911, he began to receive scholarships to study art on Saturday mornings at the art school of the John Herron Art Institute. He was just thirteen years old when he was awarded his first of those newly established scholarships. Throughout his high school years he continued to receive them.

The teachers the schoolboy encountered at Herron influenced him strongly throughout his career. Marie C. Todd (187?-1951), an Indianapolis native, was his first teacher. She had studied in New York under Arthur W. Dow, Hans Hoffman, and Robert Phillips and was graduated from the Pratt Institute. Todd's career was primarily as a teacher. She was an assistant to Wilhelmina Seegmiller, the art director in Indianapolis schools from about 1907 until 1919, when she joined the art department at Shortridge High School. There she remained until 1937.[3] Todd recommended George for the Herron scholarship program. She also instructed him at the school on Saturdays as part of that program, and her gift to him of a book of beautifully illustrated fairy tales was a deeply prized reward for his talent.[4]

But the major influence on George Mess after he entered high school in the fall of 1912 was Otto Stark (1859-1926). Stark's academic background included four years of night classes at the Cincinnati Art Academy, five years at the Art Students' League in New York, and three years in Paris at the Julian Academy. After working as a commercial artist in New York and Philadelphia upon his return from Europe, the sudden death of his wife and the needs of his four children took him back to Indianapolis. There he enjoyed a long and successful career as a teacher and fine artist.

Stark became supervisor of art at Manual Training High School in 1899. He also conducted classes at the Herron Institute after school three days a week for twenty scholarship students. George Mess was one of these. Stark has been described as "a rare teacher of art," and thousands of pupils who came under his influence went "out into the world with a better understanding of the meaning of the beautiful," which had a direct effect on their lives and the community in which they lived.[5]

The last of George Mess's Indianapolis teachers

was William Forsyth (1854-1935), with whom he studied on Saturdays during high school. Forsyth, after studying under James F. Gookins and John W. Love at the Indiana School of Art in Indianapolis, spent seven years in Munich, five of those studying at the Royal Academy (1883-1888), instructed by the Romanticists Ludwig von Loefftz and Nikolaos Gysis. After leaving the Academy he opened a studio in Munich, which he maintained for two years while also traveling in the open country and painting in Italy and in the German countryside. He returned to Indiana in 1888 and assisted in the establishment of art schools in Muncie and Fort Wayne. He also began to teach at the John Herron Institute in 1906 and elsewhere in Indianapolis. Although he won many medals for his watercolors and oils, Forsyth's metier as teacher became preeminent. "Art schools owe much to his inspiration and spirit," wrote an Indiana author, adding, "Few who have studied in Indianapolis have not come under his tutelage, which, on account of his love for youth and teaching, has been unusually successful."[6]

As his high school sketchbooks demonstrate, George Mess was a gifted teenager. When he was only sixteen years old and a junior in high school, Mess was chosen by Stark to assist in the construction of murals for the City Hospital children's ward, four floors of two units in the new building. This

George Mess poses in his army uniform, ca. 1918.

project, completed in the fall of 1914, was a remarkable landmark venture, attracting the services of every important Indiana artist of the time. Forsyth was the director of the undertaking, gathering the best painters to contribute to this monumental public work. Funded by a one thousand dollar grant from a church women's group, the St. Margaret's Guild of St. Paul's Episcopal Church, artists covered the walls with a variety of subjects executed in many styles.[7]

Stark was remembered by his fellow painters as a slow worker; he brought in George Mess to help him. Working alongside these gifted adults, the sixteen-year-old gained rapidly in self-confidence and skill. The completed murals were recognized as "the greatest undertaking thus far in the art history of the state," and George Mess had contributed to them, along with T. C. Steele, J. Ottis Adams, Wayman Adams, Clifton Wheeler, Helen Hibben, Carl Graf, and Dorothy Morlan.[8]

Along with other high school scholarship winners, Mess also participated in a project led by Stark to paint murals for the public grade school.[9]

After graduation from high school in 1916, Mess studied painting in night classes at Herron under Forsyth, and his work received immediate recognition. His painting *After the Snow* (1918) was accepted for the annual exhibits of Indiana artists at the Herron Institute. How-

George Jo Mess, *Christmas Eve*, 1936, aquatint

ever, a need to assist family finances and a desire to save enough money to go back to school full-time forced him to look for a job as well. He found one with the Western Electric Company, where he remained as a technician until 1918, when he enlisted in the United States Army. He had hoped to be shipped overseas; in his innocence he thought he would have a chance to visit the Louvre and the other museums of which he had often dreamed. But to his dismay he spent those few months before the Armistice training with his unit on the grounds of the old Butler University campus in Irvington. After being honorably discharged, he enrolled at Butler University in the fall of 1918 and supported himself by working as a laborer in a lumber and coal yard. This demanding schedule evoked a need for recreation and occasional change in the life of a young person as genial and out-going as the soft-spoken George, so he joined the national social fraternity, Delta Tau Delta.

But college life held little appeal for Mess. Only the life of the artist beckoned. After one year at Butler, without much in the way of financial backing but with a great deal of faith and hope, he rented a studio downtown on the Circle, determined to devote himself to painting. Gordon, his younger brother, was his partner almost from the beginning in the Circle Art Company, which proved to be a long and successful enterprise. Through fulfilling commercial art assignments George kept body and soul together, though he found such commissions more time-consuming than he would have preferred. But the work provided him with a means of paying his bills, and he began to develop a reputation as a commercial artist.

However, his pursuit of the labor he loved most—oil painting—was not abandoned, and after three years he had sold enough of his works and skills to take time out for more class work. He applied himself for a semester at Columbia University's Teachers College to the study of composition with the highly regarded Arthur W. Dow (1857-1922), an influential educator and a respected fine artist.[10] Mess probably went to Dow on the recommendation of his teacher Marie Todd, who as

previously noted had studied with Dow several decades before. Dow's impact on George Mess was important. Mess's later work was strongly shaped by this artist-teacher's design influence.

Teachers College at Columbia was an exciting place in the 1920s, a place for innovation and experiment that attracted many of the most original teachers and students of several generations. George Mess rented a room in a house owned by a pleasant young couple, Mr. and Mrs. Jack Whitworth. They and their little boy all became George's longtime friends. The Whitworths took him sight-seeing and introduced him to a New Yorker's New York. And, of course, he had opportunities to see some of the finest art collections in America.

George Mess returned to Indianapolis and resumed his commercial art business in the winter of 1921. He also signed up for further study with William Forsyth in evening classes at the Herron. It was during one of these classes in the autumn of 1924 that he met Evelynne Bernloehr.

Notes

1. [Will W.?] Simonds to George Mess, April 18, 1913. All manuscripts and sketchbooks cited are in possession of Evelynne Daily, unless otherwise noted.

2. Indianapolis *News*, July 15, 1908. That George, who was two years younger than Arthur, was misidentified in the article as the older brother may have reflected the fact that he was big for his age.

3. Obituary, Indianapolis *Star*, December 18, 1951.

4. Indianapolis *Star*, September 21, 1941.

5. Leland G. Howard, *Otto Stark, 1859-1926* (Indianapolis: Indianapolis Museum of Art, 1977).

6. Burnet, *Art and Artists in Indiana*, p. 175.

7. For the murals see William Forsyth, *Art in Indiana* (Indianapolis: H. Lieber Co., 1916), p. 23; Indianapolis *News*, July 4, November 28, 1914; Indianapolis *Star*, January 7, 1940. There seems to be no printed record of Mess's work on these murals. The evidence is his sketchbook.

8. Indianapolis *Star*, January 7, 1940; Burnet, *Art and Artists in Indiana*, p. 182.

9. Indianapolis Public Schools, *Annual Report*, 1916, p. 113; Indianapolis *Star*, May 14, 1919.

10. For Dow see George J. Cox, "The Horizon of A. W. Dow," *International Studio*, LXXVII (June, 1923), 189-93.

Evelynne Mess, *Branching Willow,* 1934, aquatint

Chapter 3

Getting Started,
1924-1934

THE TWO YOUNG ARTISTS were both rather shy, but their meeting, almost one of love at first sight, quickly developed into a romantic courtship and engagement. In late April, 1925, they were married. Evelynne had vowed that she would never marry "unless he's an artist," and she had kept her vow. Like the other young brides of the season, Evelynne Bernloehr Mess's photograph appeared in the *Star* in her bridal dress, but, unlike the others, she had married not just a husband but a fellow artist. From the beginning of their lives together, the lives and loves of George and Evelynne Mess were intertwined. Both embraced the other along with art, their own and each other's. "We were married to art," Evelynne reflected, "and I guess you could say art was our whole lives."

The wedding ceremony and reception were held in the bride's ancestral, high-ceilinged, music-filled house on North Alabama Street (described in glowing detail by the local papers, which rhapsodized about "a trellised arch covered with roses and honeysuckle vines [which] formed the background for the altar"). Afterwards, the young couple moved to the studio that became their permanent Indianapolis base and their home for most of their lives. Nestled in suburban Broad Ripple just north of the canal and a half mile from the trolley, it was, appropriately for people whose work was their lives, first and foremost a studio. The large, high-ceilinged front room with its large windows dominated the house.

In the next dozen years these talented young people expanded their technical skills and explored ways to make a living in art, growing ever more impatient to concentrate on their own concerns as fine artists. For most of this period George Mess continued to work in advertising art and design in his business with his brother, and this occupied a considerable part of his time. Evelynne was a freelance fashion artist for some excellent stores—the New York Store, the elegant Griffin shop (whose ads designed by Evelynne appeared in the *Columbian Magazine*), and L. S. Ayres and Company—for many of these years, but this enterprise was not very time-consuming. She also sold Christmas cards of her design nearly every year until the 1950s, often sketching friends' houses for personalized designs.

In part the contrast between George's time-consuming work and Evelynne's quickly dispatched work reflected a difference in their personal styles. Evelynne did everything allegretto. Her effervescence was apparent in every gesture, from her brisk step to her bubbling laugh. It was entirely typical of her that she saw nothing unusual about the fact that she frequently roller-skated to the grocery store, pulled along by a large pet dog. As is often the case with happily married couples, her husband was her opposite in style. As Evelynne recalled, her eyes merry with the memory of him, "he talked slowly and *moved* slowly." When he began to etch in later years, he even chose a slow-working acid. But, however deliberate George Mess may have been, he was not at all dull to live with. Extremely friendly and open, he loved to talk and was always full of plans and ideas.

In the first year of their marriage George and Evelynne, like most newlyweds, were continually struggling to earn enough to finance their new household. For one year they collaborated on producing a syndicated daily cartoon called "Doc Wise" that was published by the Western Newspaper Union. But when their contract ended, Evelynne suggested that they not renew it. She had bigger ideas. Now was the time, she felt, for her and George to do something to implement them.

Soon they began to plan the new venture. In the booming Indianapolis of the 1920s, they decided, there was room for an art school that specialized in commercial art. Obviously, their own teaching credentials were solid. But they would need a larger staff than the two of them alone represented. They gathered around them other talented young local artists: tall, handsome Elmer Taflinger (1891-1981), who had studied at the Art Students League in New York and later in Florence and had had a successful career in stage design with David Belasco;[1] Josephine Hollingsworth, a recent Herron graduate and a gifted illustrator; and George's brother Gordon (1900-1959), a student of the painter Randolph Coates. Leonard Schick, an advertising artist with whom George had worked, was another instructor.

Their school, the Circle Art Academy, opened in the fall of 1927 in three large, airy rooms, high in the old Maier-Kaiser Bank building at 128 East Washington. George and Gordon were the nominal directors, partners in this enterprise as they were in the commercial art business. Evelynne, like so many women workers in the custom of the time, was a "silent," unacknowledged partner. "George and I shared our art work, helping each other whenever we could, and that was most of the time," Evelynne recalled.

The Circle Art Academy prospered from its opening in 1927 until its closing in 1932. By 1929 there were already a great many students who had benefited from the policies of the school. In addition to being allowed to earn money while working on class projects, students were assisted in finding employment. Enrollment in George's commercial art classes boomed. Obviously, a need was being met and dealt with imaginatively. Now George's only complaint lay in his not having enough time to give to painting in his studio.

Evelynne offered fashion drawing and crafts (wood carving, block printing, leather tooling, and batik) during the first year of the school. Then, meeting the need for more space for the commercial art classes, she resigned—with some regret, perhaps, but happy in the knowledge of the success of her and George's innovation.

It would prove fortunate for them both that Evelynne now finally had an opportunity in 1928 and 1929 to pursue the goal she had set for herself years before: to master the art of etching.

By systematically telephoning local printing firms, she located an appropriate old press in 1928. By coincidence it was owned by a friend of her father's, Earl Stafford, proprietor of the Stafford Engraving Company, who agreed to let her use the abandoned press. With the equipment she had assembled—including a diamond etching needle contributed by her admiring father-in-law—she experimented with techniques learned from a textbook and brief demonstration lectures at the Herron's Print Class. In the summer of 1928, to her immense delight, the first Mess etching sprang forth and flowered before her eyes (and those of several curious Stafford employees).

Evelynne's passion for etching was confirmed by these experiments, which created a strong desire to learn her craft from a master etcher. Just as she had found her textbook on etching and a press through her own efforts, in the absence of a mentor Evelynne undertook to find a teacher on her own. Again it was the public library that provided an answer.

There Evelynne found information about the Fontainebleau School of Fine Arts in northern France, described on its letterhead as "A Summer School for American Architects, Painters, and Sculptors." The school had been started only five years before, but its faculty was a distinguished one and— most importantly—included a "graveur," an engraver of international reputation. Achile Ouvré (1872-1951) had won the Grand Prize in the Paris Exhibition of Decorative Art in 1925 and was already the illustrator of such important volumes as Mallarmé's *Poesies* and Oscar Wilde's *De Profundis.* The painters on

the faculty were equally distinguished, and so the attraction was complete. George was longing for a break from his teaching and commercial chores, and probably both artists believed that their art education would be incomplete without a period of study abroad. Thus it was that in the late fall of 1928 Evelynne applied for admission for herself and George to study the following summer in France. [2]

Before they left for France, George and Evelynne had already begun to establish themselves as important members of the Indianapolis art community. One of George's paintings was accepted for exhibit in the Hoosier Salon in 1926, only the second year of the highly successful Chicago show,

and both Evelynne and George were active members of the Indiana Artists' Club, beginning in the mid-1920s. Both exhibited paintings at the Hoosier Salon in February, 1929, and Evelynne had also exhibited a painting at the Herron Art Institute in 1928, one she had created during a brief trip to Maryland and West Virginia with George that summer (*The Narrows, Cumberland, Maryland*).[3] But the summer in France was, in retrospect, to represent a milestone in their careers, especially since it was there that Evelynne mastered the technical craft of etching.

On March 20, 1929, Evelynne received word from the New York representative of the Fontainebleau school:

We are in receipt of your letter . . . enclosing letter of recommendation and newspaper clipping. . . . On the strength of these we are ready to accept your and Mr. Mess's application for admission, and we are enclosing herewith blanks for you to fill out and return to us with check for ten dollars for each.

The three hundred dollars includes your board, lodging, and tuition. . . . Your materials would not be included but can be purchased in Paris very moderately.

We are able to secure a thirty percent discount for all our enrolled students on either the French or the Cunard lines, and the enclosed list are the boats that connect best with the opening of school, June 25th, and on which most of our students will sail. . . .

Leaving Gordon Mess in charge of the Circle Art Academy and the Circle Art Company (he was already planning that next year it would be *his* turn to study in France), the two artists set out in mid-June in high spirits. How marvelous to look forward to a summer and autumn of painting and exploring.

At Fontainebleau, working in the splendid Louis XV wing of the palace, rich in art history, the three months flew by for George and Evelynne. They both studied with landscape artists André Strauss and Gaston Balande and with the figure painter Jean Despujols, who was noted particularly for his draftsmanship. While George studied fresco wall painting with M. La Montagne Saint Subert in the palace cellars, Evelynne gloried in her self-imposed apprenticeship under Ouvré in his etching class on the third floor. Evelynne remembered him as "a charming little Frenchman with a moustache." Classes were small—no more than a dozen student etchers—and the equipment was excellent. Though he spoke no English, Ouvré communicated effectively with his eager apprentice, and she was pleased to find her reading and experimentation had provided a sound introduction to the subject. She was learning to express subtleties and refinements, qualities revealed in the portrait she etched of the beautiful operatic soprano Amelitia Galli-Curci, whom she met that summer. Evelynne remembered that her commitment to etching led her to stick a copper plate behind her sketch pads, so that even in her other classes she could steal some time to draw on the plate in preparation for etching.

Their living arrangements were something of a disappointment. The school normally arranged for its students to room with French families in the picturesque old town, and the Messes had been duly assigned to a charming apartment in a lovely home with a garden. Alas, the mattress they were provided came complete with fleas, and one night on it was all they could tolerate. The rest of their stay they roomed in a modest two-story hotel across the street from the palace. But their meals were a delight. Like all the other students at the conservatory and school of fine arts, George and Evelynne took their meals on the palace grounds in a commissary provided by the school in a very large room that seated several hundred. The food

and occasional wine were excellent and, for mid-western palates, adventuresome; Evelynne tasted her first lobster and made the aquaintance of some continental delicacies like new peas prepared in the pod. (She was so enthusiastic about French cooking that she made a personal study of the art, venturing into kitchens whenever possible for instructions from expert chefs. She published some of the results of her research in *Prairie Farmer* when she returned.)

Classes occupied most of their daylight hours and often extended into the night. Evelynne, always full of energy and never one to waste time, also joined an early morning dance class led by conservatory faculty member Henriette Brazeau a few blocks from the palace, while George worked steadily and meticulously on his sketches to improve his technique.

The landscape classes were held in the nearby Barbizon country. Twenty-five or thirty students piled onto a bus, each hauling his or her own equipment, and were deposited in a promising area where they set up their easels and began to paint. Strauss or Balande would then make his way among the students with an interpreter to criticize their work. Life drawing classes were held in classrooms in the palace. George and Evelynne got into Paris weekly to visit the major museums, for both classical and modern art.

When all too soon the three months of summer school ended, the two artists spent a few months touring and painting in the French countryside, in Switzerland and Italy, and visiting museums and cathedrals in Paris and Florence. They had planned to stay even longer and travel more, but when the stock market crashed in late October they discovered with a shock that they had lost their savings. They returned undiscouraged late that autumn to Indianapolis, refreshed and determined to apply their new skills and insights. By December, George's paintings of French landscapes—fifteen of them, with names like *Southern France*, *Across the Canal of Episy*, *Clouds of France*, and *In the Hills of Villecerf*—were on exhibition at the Pettis gallery in Indianapolis. Lucille Morehouse, the art critic of the Indianapolis *Star*, was praising the

George Jo Mess, *French Landscape*, 1929, watercolor

George Jo Mess, *Winter in Indianapolis,* 1929, oil

George Jo Mess, *Gardener's House,* 1930, watercolor

George Jo Mess, *On Tiffany's Estate*, 1931, oil

beauty of composition displayed in the paintings and rejoicing that Mess's style had not been "corrupted" by his French teachers:

It is a genuine satisfaction to find that the young Hoosier artist did not come home full of foreign mannerisms. He did not turn his back upon the sound beginning he had received in the Herron art school, but he kept it as a foundation upon which to build still further.

The exhibit appears to have been a success in other ways as well: the next time Mess exhibited his French work—in April, 1931, at the Woman's Department Club—only seven of the original fifteen paintings remained (and presumably the others had been sold).[4]

Meanwhile, among Evelynne's first acts after returning home was to purchase Mr. Stafford's old printing press. Stafford accepted her offer of a few hundred dollars, and the imposing press, with its giant wheel, would remain the focal point of the artists' possessions in their studio on Central Avenue.

Studio-home of Evelynne and George Mess, Indianapolis

George returned in the winter of 1929-1930 to the commercial art business and to teaching at his art school, enterprises that, as before, demanded nearly all of his daylight hours and that posed, therefore, serious obstacles to his painting. Evelynne's life, however, was changed somewhat in these years from its previous pattern by several factors; with the acquisition of her press she had

greater opportunities to work at etching, and she began to be drawn more into the busy world of clubs. Along with this increasing pace of activities, George and Evelynne decided that they needed a little help at home, and in solving that problem they also added another interest to their full lives. A nineteen-year-old aspiring artist named Wilbur Meese turned up in September, 1930, at the Circle Art Academy in the company of a couple from his home community in New Market, near Crawfordsville, Indiana. Meese was a protégé of a group of churchwomen, and they had raised a small sum of money to support his art education in Indianapolis. While they could not afford the Herron Art Institute, they could afford Circle Art Academy, at least for one year. Meese needed a job to earn room and board, and George immediately suggested that Meese live with him and Evelynne and perform such chores as firing the furnace and feeding pet rabbits and pigeons.

George and Evelynne were pleased with their young boarder, who became the Circle Academy's star alumnus. Evelynne remembers, "He was such a polite, clean-cut young man—so interested in all the art work we were doing." For Meese, the year was a valuable one, and he especially treasured the opportunity to share the Messes' domestic life centered around art. "I think I learned more about art from living in the home of an artist," he reflected, "than I did from the school."

Meese remembered the Mess household as an extremely lively and interesting one. He went with George and Evelynne and the Gordon Messes on sketching trips to southern Indiana in the spring and fall. Leaving very early in the morning, they enjoyed breakfast cookouts in state parks. Meese also helped Evelynne build a little pool for water lilies and goldfish in her front yard. Best of all, Meese recalls, George Mess "sat me down in his studio on Saturdays while he painted and talked to me all the time he was working, telling me what he was trying to accomplish in each painting." Meese considered these free art lessons a tremendous gift.

While George taught Meese painting, Evelynne was like "a second mother," Meese says. Fresh off the farm, the young Meese knew no one in Indi-

Evelynne Mess, *Amelitia*, 1930, drypoint

anapolis. "Evelynne encouraged me to go to church and make friends. She took care of me and helped me get started in art." Meese later went on to successful careers both as a commercial artist and as a fine artist, especially in watercolors.[5]

Despite the demands of earning a living by his teaching and commercial assignments and despite the obstacles of his own slow pace and quest for perfection, George Mess managed to produce paintings that were accepted for important exhibits in the first years after his return from Europe. European scenes as subject matter evidently did not appeal to George, who preferred to record people and places close to home. In what free time he could find, usually in the evenings, he painted daily life as he knew it in Indianapolis and surrounding areas. His work proceeded slowly, not only because of other demands on his time, but because of his self-imposed commandments for perfection. His ideals, stern taskmasters, always led him to greater efforts.

In the fall of 1930 his landscape painting *Winter in Indianapolis* was exhibited at an international exhibition at the Carnegie Institute in Pittsburgh (one of only forty-eight American paintings accepted from more than twelve hundred submitted). The following year, 1931, two landscapes, *Indianapolis in Snow* and *Brookside Bridge*, were shown at the Cincinnati Art Museum in its Thirty-eighth Annual Exhibition of American Art, and closer to home his work was recognized by two important institutions: the Indianapolis Art Association, which awarded his painting *Metamora* its annual $150 prize at the Herron Institute's Indiana Artists Exhibit, and the Indiana Artists' Club, which awarded George the prize for work produced by an artist thirty-five years old or younger.[6]

Early in March, 1931, a letter from Oyster Bay, New York, reached George's desk. "The Louis Comfort Tiffany Foundation will open its twelfth season as a residence for artists on May the first, and I am anxious to have your cooperation in the selection of desirable candidates," wrote the director of this prestigious institution founded in 1919 by the son of the famous Manhattan jeweler and stained-glass artist. "The foundation," he continued,

accepts artists who meet its requirements in painting, sculpture and craft-work, although painters usually predominate in number. It is in no sense a school, and no instruction will be offered. Candidates, therefore, must show both considerable talent and sufficient technical training to be able to carry on their work without assistance. Artists prominent in various fields will visit the Foundation from time to time for the purpose of giving constructive criticism.

Our aim is to encourage individual thought rather than to stand for a particular viewpoint, and we hope thus eventually to do something toward the furtherance of a distinctive quality in American art.

. . . I am sending you our prospectus for the present season, and I shall be grateful if you will bring it to the attention of such artists as would be interested in joining our group. . . .[7]

George tacked the letter to the school's bulletin board and urged some of the students to apply. Both he and Evelynne applied immediately and submitted original examples of their work. The jury accepted George as a Tiffany fellow but rejected Evelynne, on the ground that "the Foundation never admits married couples."

It was an important achievement for George. The Tiffany judges had placed him among the most promising and original young artists in the country. He spent the summer painting the Oyster Bay landscape and exchanging ideas with fellow artists. As promised, some leading artists of the time—including Gifford R. Beal, the landscape and figure painter, and Luigi Lucioni, the noted etcher of New England landscapes—visited the Tiffany Fellows to offer criticisms.

But the judges' failure to admit Evelynne was a disappointment for both her and George. They were thus condemned to several months of separation—and it was a disquieting instance of being placed in competition with one another. The thought occurred to Evelynne that it was not fair to be penalized for being the wife of an artist.

Evelynne's work since their return from Europe in the fall of 1929 had been focused on etching, and she produced many prints inspired by the sketching trips she had made in Europe. While her preferred technique would later be to sketch directly onto the plate without preliminary working drawings, in the first years of her etching career she worked from the wealth of sketches she had accumulated during their months in France. (Only *Rainy Day in Fontainebleau, Montmarte,* and *Old Montmarte* were etched in France; the other European subjects were etched at home, from sketches.) The first exhibition of her European etchings appears to have been at the Hoosier Salon in Chicago in March, 1931, where she showed *Rainy Day in Fontainebleau, Trees of Fontainebleau, Towers of the Alps,* and *Porte de Samois.* But she was also working on some new ideas, such as those demonstrated in the bookplate etching she showed at the State Fair in 1930 and the *Water Fantasy* she showed at the Society of American Etchers in New York at the end of 1931. Meanwhile, in 1930, in addition to etching, running her household, and frequent teaching as a 'substitute' in the Indianapolis schools (all of which she carried

on for many years), she began teaching an etching class and formed a club for etchers.[8]

During that lonely summer of 1931, Evelynne also began to be involved in a time-consuming way in yet another "career," that of a clubwoman working to promote art. Beginning in 1931 she was recruited for women's club work by the doyenne of Indiana art patrons, Mary Quick Burnet (Mrs. Henry B., 1863-1938), and Burnet's younger colleague Katherine McLeod Smith (Mrs. Leonidas F., 1885-1974).

Burnet was an important leader in the Indianapolis women's club movement generally, as one of the founders in 1912 of the activist Indianapolis Woman's Department Club, and a model citizen leader of the Progressive era, with interests that ranged from children's aid to smoke abatement. But her special expertise was in the fine arts, and she was the major force in organizing women to support the arts in the early decades of the century.

The Fresco Studio in the Palace of Fontainebleau was considered the finest in the world when George Jo and Evelynne Mess studied there in the summer of 1929. George is seated on the scaffold at left; standing next to him is Montaigne Saint Subert, head of the school's fresco department.

Evelynne Mess, *Towers of the Alps*, 1930, etching

The Art Department of the Indianapolis Woman's Department Club was her creation, with its regular exhibits, lectures, classes in art history, and collection of pictures by Indiana artists available for rental or sale. Burnet also founded statewide organizations to promote art—the Indiana Federation of Art Clubs and the Hoosier Salon Patrons Association—and was a power in the arts division of the Indiana General Federation of Women's Clubs. Educated in the Columbus, Indiana, public schools, at Purdue, and the Indianapolis Art School, Burnet had published the still useful *Art and Artists of Indiana* in 1921 and was a highly respected figure in Indiana art circles.[9]

Katherine Smith was a younger version of Burnet and became heir to her leadership in Indiana art clubs when Burnet died suddenly in 1938. Though Mrs. Smith, a Shortridge graduate with a business school background, lacked Mrs. Burnet's training in art history, she compensated by becoming the art club's best student and served the movement assiduously until the 1960s.[10]

Evelynne was discovered by these dynamic leaders by 1931. (Mrs. Burnet entertained at a lawn party in June, partly to highlight Evelynne's work and that of her students, hanging the pictures from clotheslines.) Within the following year, Evelynne was persuaded to lend her expertise to the Art Department of the Indianapolis Woman's Department Club. She served several years as chairman of the important Exhibits Committee (1933-1934, 1935-1936, and 1936-1937). Evelynne was also asked by the younger members of the department (the "Little Club") to become their art director. She set up a gallery on the third floor of the clubhouse and also offered lessons in arts and crafts to members. The young artist was also active in the department's garden section (and was its first secretary), and her influence was felt in various club programs in these years (George was featured in a club lecture in 1933, and the lecture on etching in 1934-1935 was probably her doing).[11]

Club work was demanding and time-consuming, but Evelynne Mess never lacked energy. And in positive terms, club work gave her an opportunity to reach an adult audience, i.e., essentially to teach on a higher level than that of high school and serve the cause of art through her ability to organize exhibits. Evelynne Mess was a friendly and gracious young matron who enjoyed the company of other attractive and intelligent women. (That she also saw some of the more humorous aspects of women's clubs became clear in a prize-winning painting she produced in 1948, *Committee Women*, years after she had resigned from the Woman's Department Club.)

George and Evelynne's lives began to change in other ways in the 1930s. The Circle Art Academy had by this time lost what little enchantment such a responsibility had ever held for George. Aware of his brother's discontent, Gordon Mess and four colleagues persuaded him to agree to closing the art school in 1932 and join in establishing the Circle Engraving Company. Although his position as head of the commercial art department of the company guaranteed a regular salary, he soon discovered that he had only succeeded in exchanging the frustrations of one occupation for the dead weight of another. He still had not gained the freedom he so greatly deserved to devote to painting. Also, he would soon realize that his naive commitment to the new enterprise would prove to be a financial disaster.

The following year was a difficult one for George and Evelynne. Both Joseph Mess and John Bernloehr died in 1933 at the depth of the Great Depression. Joseph Mess died in April at age sixty-two, and John Bernloehr died in August at age fifty-nine. The loss of either parent—so loving and supportive—would have been a blow to these young artists, the loss of both fathers within a single year, devastating.

However, the early 1930s did offer some more positive milestones in their careers. George won first prizes for oil painting and for watercolor at the Indiana State Fair in 1932, and he was selected to represent Indiana—along with nineteen other "widely known Indiana artists"—at the Chicago Century of Progress Exposition in 1933. In 1934—along with Evelynne, Gordon, and a dozen other Indiana artists—George was accorded the honor of a solo exhibition of his paintings at the John Her-

Evelynne Mess, *Grossmunster Cathedral*, 1930, etching

ron Art Institute.[12]

But for Evelynne this period was even more productive. At the same time her club work was expanding, her reputation as a printmaker was growing. Her work in this field was shown at the annual Indiana Artists' Exhibit at the Herron Art Institute in 1932, 1933, and 1934. The year 1934 was a triumphant one for Evelynne; her etchings were exhibited in important shows across the country—Los Angeles County Art Museum, the Society of American Etchers (later the Society of American Graphic Artists) in New York (for the second year in a row), and the Pennsylvania Academy of Fine Art. At the Hoosier Salon in 1934, five of Evelynne's prints were accepted for exhibit. And she was invited to mount a solo show at the Herron Art Institute in February, where she exhibited both the etchings she had created in Europe and the etchings, aquatints, and block prints she had created since 1929. This was followed by another solo show at the Fort Wayne Art School in April. She created more than a dozen prints in 1934; it was the most productive year of her printmaking career.[13]

Perhaps the most extraordinary element in this burst of accomplishment was Evelynne's organization of the Indiana Society of Printmakers. Having observed the flourishing of clubs and societies of printmakers elsewhere, Evelynne reasoned the time had come to establish such an organization in Indiana. Artists in the field would enjoy meeting with one another occasionally to socialize and exchange ideas. And indeed they would welcome an opportunity to show their work. In January, 1934, singlehandedly, she organized the original twenty-five-member Indiana Society of Printmakers, whose first exhibition was held that same year at the Lieber galleries in Indianapolis.[14] The exhibit received enthusiastic praise. Wrote Beatrice Burgan, woman's editor of the Indianapolis *Times*,[15]

It was a happy thought of Evelynne Mess when she invited Frederick Polley and Loreen Wingerd to her studio in January for the purpose of doing something about organizing print makers in Indiana. Never before has Indianapolis been given such an opportunity to see the work of its print makers, whose society has given impetus to their activities. . . . Study of the prints brings deeper appreciation. Every line, every gradation of tone are indispensable to the artists' executions. . . .

Evelynne began immediately making plans to send members' prints to shows held periodically throughout the state. She corresponded with every printmaker she could find who was born in Indiana or who lived and worked there. In addition, and again through correspondence, she synchronized traveling exhibits so that expenses—and shipping problems, if any—remained at a minimum. Prints traveled around the state via parcel post in a hinged box she designed and built and to which she attached a handle for the postman's convenience. With zest and love she served the cause of printmaking in Indiana for over twenty years, thereby inspiring a whole generation of artists who otherwise might never have discovered they possessed talent in so specialized a field.

Not only were the lives of artists and art students enriched through her commitment. She also helped to deepen the insight of gallery-goers, collectors, and art lovers in general as they perceived that their interests could readily embrace yet another sphere.

Paramount to the traveling exhibitions was, of course, the annual spring show in Indianapolis presented either at Lieber's or the Herron. Regarding the 1936 exhibit, Lucille Morehouse, reviewer for the Indianapolis *Star*, commented that those persons "who have worked loyally to boost the state's art movement will certainly be rejoiced over the work that is being done by the talented and sincere group of artists who are interpreting beauty through the medium of black and white prints. . . ."[16]

Evelynne was to remain the Indiana Society of Printmakers' mainstay for many years. It is clear that her ingenuity in solving the practical problems of moving art works safely and efficiently and her organizational skills in mounting exhibits were important assets to the Society throughout its life.[17]

Notes

1. Clippings, 1930, Evelynne Mess Daily scrapbook, pp. 69, 75 (hereafter cited EMD scrapbook).

2. For Fontainebleau School see *American Magazine of Art*, XXI (July 1930), 403-404.

3. Indianapolis *News*, August 3, 1928.

4. Indianapolis *Star*, December 22, 1929, April 19, 1931. Much of what they painted and etched remained behind in Europe, since their work was simply too bulky for them to bring it all home. Many canvasses were given to friends— either to keep or to paint over. Something else that was left behind was the name 'Evelyn.' The French version suited Evelynne much better, and she adopted it thereafter.

5. Wilbur Meese interview, July 29, 1983.

6. Pittsburgh *Post Gazette*, October 3, 1930; Indianapolis *Star*, March 1, 8, 1931. Lucille Morehouse disapproved of George's landscape because she found it to be a "formula" French landscape.

7. Director of Louis Comfort Tiffany Foundation to George Mess, Circle Art Academy, March, 1931.

8. Indianapolis *Star*, November 22, 1931.

9. *Women's Who's Who*, 1914-1915, s.v. "Burnet, Mary Q."; Indianapolis *Star*, September 7, 1938.

10. Indianapolis *Star*, September 7, 1974.

11. Indianapolis *News*, June 11, 1931; Indianapolis Woman's Department Club *Yearbook*, 1932-1933, 1933-1934, 1934-1935, 1935-1936, 1936-1937; Indianapolis *Star*, December 14, 1934.

12. Indianapolis *Star*, September 4, 1932; Indianapolis *News*, March 31, 1933; Art Association of Indianapolis, Indiana, *Annual Report*, 1934-1935, pp. 13, 20.

13. Indianapolis *News*, February 16, 1934; Ft. Wayne *Journal*, April 24, 1934; clipping, December, 1934, EMD scrapbook, p. 39.

14. Indianapolis *News*, January 6, 1934.

15. Indianapolis *Times*, June 1, 1934.

16. Indianapolis *Star*, May 24, 1936.

17. For a more complete analysis of the Indiana Society of Printmakers see below, pp. 103-114.

George Jo Mess, *Ed Lucky's Farm*, 1937, aquatint

Chapter 4

New Directions,
1935-1940

THE LIVES OF GEORGE AND EVELYNNE changed dramatically in the second half of the 1930s, primarily because George developed an interest in etching. This was due in large measure to a request made to Evelynne for sketches of the interior of the old Fauntleroy house in New Harmony, Indiana. While interested in, and supportive of, his wife's work in printmaking, George had not, previous to joining the sketching trip to New Harmony, thought about learning etching himself. While Evelynne was dashing from room to room in the old house, recording in pen and ink the required scenes, George composed a pencil drawing of a backyard view along one of the village streets, intending to make a painting of it.

"I could just see that sketch being made into an etching," Evelynne recalls, "because the composition, the subject matter—everything was all absolutely right for the medium. So I said, 'Why don't you make an etching of that, George? I know you can do it—your draftsmanship, your perfectionism, all the things you do so well are just right for learning etching. And we have all the equipment. I can teach you what I know.'" And so George began his lessons with Evelynne, his only instructor in this art, in 1934.

Ostensibly Mess's rise to success as a printmaker seems to have sprung from nowhere, like a wild rose that suddenly volunteers its plantings along a garden wall. But his triumph may be described more correctly as a breakthrough resulting from past hours of diligence on the part of this talented artist seeking perfection at the drawing board and easel. Furthermore, his wife's etching techniques, long observed by him, had undoubtedly permeated his unconsciousness so fully that his feeling for cre-

ating in the medium seemed to reach him by a kind of osmosis. As George Jo Mess experimented with his first etching, he really already knew how to create one.

"George was always interested in tone values rather than line, so aquatint was the natural medium for him," Evelynne recalls. Much of the development of his technique depended upon patiently experimenting with timing and various acids to achieve different tonal effects, and this experimentation Evelynne left to George, since this interested him much more than it did her. But the original instruction and all the equipment and materials were supplied by Evelynne, along with warm encouragement and moral support.

A full description of George's aquatint technique appeared in an article published in 1945. From it, comes the following:[1]

> An aquatint is an etching of tones, developed from a porous ground, which gives a wash-drawing effect. When this process is successfully handled, it produces prints of great depth and richness of tone.

> First, powdered resin is dusted onto the surface of a copper plate which is then heated enough to melt the particles of resin and make them adhere to the metal. When the plate, thus treated, is immersed in an acid bath, the bath will etch only in the minute spaces between the acid-resisting particles of resin. A plate treated in this manner will print—when inked—a flat textured tone. How dark it will be depends upon the length of time it has remained in the acid, consequently how far the etching has proceeded.

> Any areas of design that are to remain pure white are covered, before etching begins, with a stopping-out varnish to prevent etching of those parts.

We now have a plate that will print one flat gray, except for certain white areas. To produce a darker tone on parts of the plate, apply stopping-out varnish to the white areas and those which should be light gray in the print. The acid bath will then further etch the remaining parts and darken their tones. It will be seen that this stopping-out and re-etching process can be repeated as many times as desired, producing an infinite number of tones in the finished aquatint print.

George went on to describe in detail his own preferred techniques and timings, though he noted that "each design may require different timings, and after keeping notes on the first few plates one will readily find a correct timing sense to suit his own needs." Almost as an afterthought he added, "Often I use as many as sixteen or seventeen stages and etchings on one plate." George's approach to the medium was meticulous and systematic:

> I keep records of all stagings, etching times and number of dustings on the side margin of my original sketch for future reference. I try to etch the tones of one dusting in one day for if the plate has small amounts of iron left on it overnight, further biting will occur. When the etching is clearly bitten, and care has been taken throughout the process, the plate will produce several hundred good prints.

George later recalled the impact of encountering etchings and drawings by Whistler and Speicher in museums that he and Evelynne visited in Cincinnati and Louisville while on vacation in 1935. But most of that trip was spent in a leisurely sketching tour of the Blue Mountains and then along the Ohio River. From these sketches George made many of his earliest etchings: *Metamora, Summertime, Gardener's House, The Open Road,* and *Edge of the Forest.* Altogether George created a dozen etchings in 1935.[2]

George's approach to printmaking was quite different from Evelynne's. For one thing, as noted earlier, he worked almost exclusively with aquatints, whereas Evelynne worked with many other media: etching (her favorite), dry point, lithographs, and woodcuts, as well as aquatint. George perfected his composition as a detailed drawing before transferring it to a copper plate by careful trac-

ing. Even though Evelynne made a number of etchings based upon her sketches, her preferred approach was more spontaneous, a freehand drawing directly upon the plate. George was primarily interested in the tonal possibilities of aquatint, so his technique was built around slow-acting acids, like iron perchloride (it took up to an hour to etch the deepest tones), that could be carefully controlled for precise effects. Evelynne was usually most interested in line and preferred fast-acting acids, like nitric acid, that achieved the lines she wanted quickly. And while both were landscape and nature artists, they were strikingly different in their products.

Etching is an extremely confining, time-consuming undertaking even for those whose techniques are like Evelynne's. For George, who took a meticulous approach to an already demanding medium, etching would presumably have been a prohibitively difficult undertaking if it had not been for the technical assistance he received from the beginning from Evelynne. Often she traced his completed drawings onto the copper plates and, following his detailed instructions, applied and removed the slow-working acids, timing them carefully. Although she tried several times to train students to prepare the prints for the press—which takes from fifteen to twenty minutes per print—she was never successful in doing this to her own satisfaction and so often found herself left with this complex and time-consuming task. First the paper must be soaked; then the ink is mixed and rubbed into the plate; then the plate must be carefully wiped, leaving the ink in the etched places; then the paper is blotted and dried; and lastly the plate is printed on the paper. When one considers that this process is repeated perhaps fifty to a hundred times per etching, one begins to perceive what a tremendous labor Evelynne performed to help her husband as a printmaker.

Evelynne's productivity as a printmaker began to decline as George's exploded. George created more than a hundred aquatints in the half-dozen years from 1935 to 1941—more than Evelynne has etched in her long lifetime as a printmaker. But it is also clear that George's career as a printmaker

George Jo Mess, *A Century of Progress*, 1932, oil

George Jo Mess, *Along White River*, 1934, oil

George Jo Mess, *Backyard Romance*, 1937, oil

George Jo Mess, *Garden of Eve*, 1937, aquatint

George and Evelynne work at the etching press in their Central Avenue studio.

during this period was heavily dependent upon his wife's assistance. He was, it will be recalled, working full-time as a commercial artist. Evelynne put it simply, "He was always working." There was no independent income, no patron. George earned their living by his commercial work as an artist throughout the decade of the Great Depression, and it left him little leisure for his own creative work. He was prolific in ideas for etchings and in designing them, but it was Evelynne's willingness to do much of the tedious technical work that enabled him to make a career as a printmaker. It was not, as Evelynne makes clear, that he could not do his own etching. He was a skilled and innovative etcher with strong convictions about how to achieve the effects he wanted. But he did not have time in the early years to follow through by himself with all the details.

Evelynne's own work in these years continued to win considerable attention. Her *Lilies of the Field* (1936), for example, won a place in the *American Block Print Calendar* for 1937, alongside the work of Thomas Hart Benton, Stuart Davis, Rockwell Kent, and Grant Wood. Of the one hundred printmakers asked to contribute, only fifty-three were represented in the publication.[3] But Evelynne's work on George's etchings entailed a sacrifice of her own work. It was, by her own account, a sacrifice that she was willing to make, both because of her personal devotion to the man and because of her pride in George Mess the artist.

It was a choice that apparently did not worry her at the time, though, prodded by the present-day woman's movement, she has in recent years wondered whether it was the right one. And, while George was deeply proud of his wife and did what he could to help her in her career as an artist, it is also true that he accepted her sacrifice without protest, perhaps even complacently, with a traditional man's unexamined conviction that when a married couple's individual interests conflicted, it was right that the man should prevail.

These were not explicit issues for Evelynne and George Mess. Evelynne was extremely quick and ready to be helpful; George was ponderous and always in need of help. It was a partnership in which each gave what he/she could. In the late 1930s George's contribution was to hold down some challenging jobs and design etchings that brought national recognition; Evelynne contributed much of her time and expertise to helping him execute his etchings and print them.

George Mess's experiments with aquatint in the fall and winter of 1935-1936 were dramatically successful. Before the end of the year, some of his earliest efforts (*Aurora* and *Edge of the Forest*) were accepted for major exhibits in Philadelphia and New York. In February, 1936, nine aquatint etchings were exhibited at the Hoosier Salon in Chicago and won the Frank Cunningham Prize for best prints. Meanwhile, *Aurora* had been chosen by the Philadelphia Society of Etchers to be included in their annual traveling exhibit, and by March there were other George Mess prints on exhibit at the National Academy of Design in New York and the Seattle Art Museum. Elisabeth Luther Cary, art critic of the New York *Times*, found George's *The Barren Plum Tree* (1935) to be one of the two most impressive prints in the Philadelphia Print Club Show in April, 1936, and was especially struck by the aquatint's "delicate transitions."

The print is not large and the smaller branches of the tree are slender, but none of them too slender for the introduction of a quiet half-tone against the heavier darks giving weight and depth to the sturdy structure of the tree. The incident of the small

Evelynne Mess, *Nature's Lacework*, 1935, aquatint-etching

Evelynne Mess, *Winding Road*, 1935, aquatint-etching

Evelynne Mess, *Rooster*, 1935, blockprint

Evelynne Mess, *Lilies of the Field*, 1936, woodcut

buildings down in one corner, the sun bright upon their walls, the stream that runs silver in the distance, the bank reflected in its shining surface—the whole beauty of the scene restrained yet opulent— a grand little picture.

He was immediately elected to membership in the Philadelphia Society of Printmakers and the Northwest Printmakers.[4]

By the end of 1936 *Backyard Romance* had proved that the new etcher was no fluke. This striking aquatint based on his New Harmony sketch was first exhibited in major shows in New York and Philadelphia, then selected by the American Artists Alliance as one of the 100 Prints of the Year for exhibit first in New York and then in thirty major cities with eventual publication as *America Today*. His *Abode of the Boatmaker* was also accepted for the International Exhibit of Etching and Engraving at the Chicago Art Institute in the fall of 1936.[5]

George J. Mess, vice-president of Circle Engraving, member of the Columbia Club, officer of the Universal Club, and board member of the Carrollton Avenue Reformed Church, continued to make a living as a commercial artist, while Evelynne kept on with her multiple roles of artist, wife, and clubwoman/teacher. But as George J. Mess began to be perceived more as George Jo Mess, the nationally acclaimed fine artist, he grew more frustrated by the continuing need to turn out advertising art in order to support his work in fine art. Fortunately, he discussed his feelings with his friend L. L. Goodman. Goodman and his brother Jack owned the Real Silk Hosiery Company, a large and successful Indianapolis business. George had designed and painted advertisements for the Goodmans for many years, and they and their families had developed warm friendships. The Goodmans bought George's and Evelynne's paintings and commissioned the couple to paint murals in their houses. In the course of this latter project, Goodman probed the subject of George's dissatisfaction with his work. Asked to describe the kind of work he would most like to be doing, George replied that he wanted time to work at his own art. He did not object to a nine-to-five job, so long as he was being paid to make prints and to paint.

Remarkably, L. L. Goodman knew of an opening that satisfied most of George's wishes and was eager to help his friend to move into it. It was a stroke of fortune that turned the Messes' lives in an entirely new direction.

The position in question was on the staff of Esquire, Incorporated, as artist and technical director for *Esquire*, *Apparel Arts*, and *Coronet*. All of these magazines (and later *Ken*, which appeared from April, 1938, to August, 1939) were published in Chicago by a dynamic young tycoon named David Smart (1892-1952), who happened to be a friend of L. L. Goodman. *Esquire* was highly successful from the start with its mixture of the irreverent, the risqué, and the fashionable, with a prestigious overlay of work by serious artists. Buoyed by his successes, Smart also began to publish a "pocket-sized" journal. *Coronet*, which appeared in November, 1936, was an ambitious magazine in its early days, publishing fine art and imaginative literature along with short articles on a wide variety of subjects.

David Smart was one of the most exciting figures in the world of publishing in 1937. His magazines were successful, and he was publishing a remarkable quantity of contemporary art in a popular context.

Smart was immediately interested in Mess. The one requirement he made was that George submit a portfolio of nudes to demonstrate that he could do bodies as well as landscapes. The result was a stunning group of aquatints—all featuring the lovely Evelynne.

The two artists left Indianapolis in July, 1937, with the spirit of adventure and confidence of talented people on their way up. The change in their lives was abrupt and dramatic. They left their lifelong home, their families and friends—a familiar world where they were liked, admired, and respected—and entered a high-pressure city life. They rented out the Central Avenue house and moved to a studio occupying one floor of a three-story building on Wabash Avenue near the Esquire offices, so that George could walk to work.

George's responsibilities were engrossing. He was to oversee the technical reproduction of all the art work in all of Smart's magazines. The mass pro-

George Jo Mess, *Southern Oak*, 1936, aquatint

George Jo Mess, *Chicago*, 1938, aquatint

duction of fine art was a considerable challenge, and the job was demanding. While some of his work involved retouching other artists' products to achieve the most successful reproductions, most of his job was illustrating texts with pen-and-ink drawings. Mess was also called upon almost monthly to produce original prints to illustrate poems. *Esquire* published a large portfolio of his aquatints in a special section of the magazine in January, 1938, to introduce their new staff member.

The Messes entered their new life with enthusiasm. Chicago's art world offered exciting new experiences for them. George and Evelynne attended Bauhaus lectures in the evenings, and Evelynne spent her days exploring the city. During her three years in Chicago, Evelynne studied lithography at the Art Institute of Chicago, ceramics at Hull

House, lapidary at the Academy of Science, and photography at the Eastman School.

But the move to Chicago was not without its perils for Evelynne. In Indianapolis she had her own independent identity as an artist and clubwoman; in Chicago, at first at least, she was just George's wife. Her friend Katherine (Mrs. Leonidas F.) Smith, director of the Hoosier Salon, wrote Evelynne soon after the move to Chicago, tactfully addressing that problem. But Mrs. Smith's intended reassurance that Evelynne was doing a splendid job by helping George (and comparing her with the wives of Wayman Adams and J. Ottis Adams) may have also served to discourage her somewhat. Much more helpful for Evelynne's morale were the duo exhibits Mrs. Smith arranged for the two artists in 1938 and 1939 at the Hoosier Salon Art Gallery in Chicago, firmly establishing

George Jo Mess, *In My Studio*, 1937, aquatint

George Jo Mess, *Locket for a Very Young Girl*, 1938, aquatint

George Jo Mess, *Rural Delivery*, 1937, aquatint

George Jo Mess, *Wishing Gate*, 1937, aquatint

Evelynne's separate identity as a fine artist for the Chicago art world.[6] Whether it was these pressures or simply the unaccustomed noise of Chicago (and the fact that the roadbed for the elevated trains was being constructed near their studio), Evelynne began to suffer from migraine headaches soon after their move to Chicago.

However, the Chicago years were immensely productive ones for both George and Evelynne, though Evelynne's contributions were not always publicly recognized. George created nearly seventy etchings—almost half of his lifetime production—during the four years from January, 1937, through 1940. While he never "knock[ed] off thirty etchings a year," as the *Esquire* copywriter breezily claimed in the article and portfolio of his etchings published by the magazine in January, 1938, he did turn out about twenty per year in three of the four years. He accomplished this feat, morever, while working very hard for the Esquire company's several magazines. The key to his ability to work eight or ten hours a day for Esquire and then produce richly detailed aquatints at home in the evenings and weekends was again his wife's extensive technical assistance. Evelynne essentially abandoned her own etching during this period; she produced two during the four-year period [*Wren's Gourd House* (1939) and *Toadstools* (1940)]. Most of her own work was done as woodcuts and lithographs. While she *was* doing a great deal of etching, it was not her own work; she was laboring long and hard as George's helper for the monthly *Coronet* prints—tracing his drawings onto copper plates, applying and timing acids according to his instructions, and printing the proofs after he approved them.

Perhaps because George was rushing to turn out so much during these years and also perhaps because he was far from the natural landscapes that inspired him, relatively little that he created during these hectic times remains in permanent collections. His most admired aquatints from these years were created either before he went to Chicago or during the times he was away from there: *Ed Luckey's Farm*, *Ever So Humble* (which was exhibited at the Paris International Exhibition in 1937), and

Wishing Gate, all produced in 1937 before he went to Chicago; *Reelsfoot Bridge*, *Time for Rest*, *If Winter Comes*, *Work-shed*, *Coastline*, and *Bayfield*, produced in 1939 while he was recuperating from surgery; and *Old Fairland Mill* and *Sand Dune Cabins*, produced in 1940, while on vacation.

The fact was that George Jo Mess was a landscape artist and never in his element in the big city—whether it was Chicago or Indianapolis. While he created some striking city landscapes (the painting *Winter in Indianapolis* that had been shown at the international exhibit in Pittsburgh, for example, and the aquatint *City of Rooftops*), the subjects that moved him most were rustic farms on which people lived close to nature.

Evelynne, too, was an artist most deeply moved and most often inspired by natural subjects. Aside from the European village scenes that formed the basis for much of her work for a decade after she returned from France, Evelynne's preferred subjects were natural objects and creatures and landscapes.

But while they may have been somewhat out of their element artistically during their years in Chicago, socially George and Evelynne had the time of their lives. They were warm, gregarious people with a large capacity for fun as well as for hard work. They quickly formed a congenial part of the Esquire circle of staff artists, including Tony Palazzo, Eric Lundgren, and William Sharp. The two artists brought Palazzo and his wife back to Indiana with them for painting weekends, and sometimes stayed with the Lundgrens for similar weekends on the Dunes. Evelynne recalls that she taught Sharp how to etch. Dave Smart was enthusiastic about the Messes and continually drew them into his own social life. A youngish bachelor "man-about-town" with film-star good looks and a taste for the "good life," Smart swept George and Evelynne off to ball games and George to boxing matches and asked them to serve as cohost and hostess for his own entertainments in his various residences (an apartment at the Drake Hotel, a penthouse at the top of the Palmolive Building, and a house in the country). Through Smart the Messes

Evelynne Mess, *Nightclub Lights*, 1938, lithograph

George Jo Mess, *The Hitching Post*, 1938, aquatint

met many of the country's leading writers and artists, some of whom—like Ernest Hemingway and John Dos Passos—were frequent contributors to *Esquire*. While spending the weekends at Smart's country house—which featured both a swimming pool and a large circular bed that rotated when a button was pushed to reveal various views of natural scenery from a large wraparound window—George and Evelynne enjoyed a life far removed from the simple, work-centered existence they had known in Indianapolis.

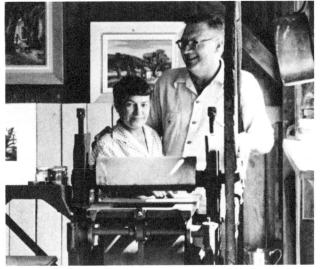

Almost from the beginning of their sojourn in Chicago, Evelynne's and George's sociability and inherent civility combined to bring them many friends both inside and outside of the art world. People found the modest, unpretentious pair attractive, admired their art work and generally enjoyed being in the company of a married couple whose congeniality spilled over into other lives. Clearly, the two artists basked in the respect and love each felt for the other. Not often, if ever, had their friends met a husband-wife artist team whose marriage could survive without succumbing to competitiveness and jealousy in the field they shared—or indeed could survive at all. While it is true that Evelynne was often to become the unsung partner, she knew that in spirit she was a great deal more, both in George's mind and heart and in a solemn, fundamental way of living she would soon be forced to experience.

In 1939 George became ill and doctors discovered that he had cancer. The Chicago surgeon had not been acquainted with the couple before an operation revealed the cause of the artist's illness, but evidently he was acquainted with the artistic temperament. At least the advice he offered to Evelynne in George's case proved to be the right kind to give.

And so George was not told of his condition. How successful the ruse was is not clear. His very slow and incomplete recovery from surgery undoubtedly alarmed and depressed him. Still, when he went with Evelynne and her sister and brother-in-law to Ghost Lake, a little Wisconsin lake near Lake Superior, to recuperate for a few weeks after the operation, George was as productive an artist as ever; he made drawings for at least four aquatints.

George struggled along after the operation for many months and even tried to return for a short time to the *Esquire-Coronet* job. By July, 1940, nearly a year after his surgery, it was clear that the demands of the position were sapping his diminished reserves of strength. Finally, Evelynne and the surgeon convinced George to give up the job and take on an easier life-style. In the late summer of 1940, exactly three years from the time they had left Indianapolis, they were back in their house and studio on Central Avenue.

Notes

1. Ernest Watson, "A Hoosier Artist: George Jo Mess," in *American Artist*, IX (June, 1945), 14-19, 30.

2. Indianapolis *Times*, February 27, 1936.

3. Indianapolis *Star*, December 20, 1936; *Who is Who in the American Block Print Calendar 1937*, EMD scrapbook, p. 35.

4. *Columbian*, XII (February, 1936), p. 15; New York *Times*, April 19, 1936; Indianapolis *News*, March 26, 1936.

5. Indianapolis *Times*, November 27, 1936; New York *Times*, December 13, 1936.

6. Indianapolis *Star*, April 5, 1938; Chicago *Herald Examiner*, April 24, 1938; Chicago *Tribune*, June 12, 1939.

George Jo Mess, *Self Portrait*, 1940, aquatint

Chapter 5

Home:
1940-1962

GEORGE AND EVELYNNE came back to Indiana to stay in 1940. But while they returned to their former home, they did not return to their former lives. Once again the two artists began to construct a new life together. While many aspects of that life were to vary in the years to come, its basic structure was a durable one. After 1940 George never again earned his living primarily as a commercial artist; he was now committed to a life as a fine artist. Much of the success and achievement of this career—especially after his first operation in 1939—was attributable to the assistance and promotion contributed by Evelynne. After the first year, George turned his attention away from etching and back to painting. After 1941 George Jo Mess was primarily a painter and only occasionally an etcher. And in the mid-1940s George developed a new career as a teacher of fine art that flourished and grew until the end of his life.

Evelynne's life after their return to Indianapolis was devoted primarily to keeping George alive and happy (i.e., working). "I never knew how long he would last, and I felt he had so much to give. I just worked as hard as I could to encourage him and to promote his work." Her triumph was that despite several operations between 1939 and 1962, George Mess lived twenty-three years after his first operation and was a productive artist until the end.

Evelynne's achievement was not accomplished without cost to her own career. Much of her time and energy after 1939 was devoted literally to nursing her husband back to health. And even when his physical health was relatively good by the mid-1940s, Evelynne continued to devote herself to helping George pursue *his* career as an artist.

She was cheerful about this sacrifice for several reasons. For one thing, Evelynne was (and is) cheerful about most things. For another, she believed in George and was confident that he deserved her devotion. And lastly, it never occurred to her that there was any alternative to this course; she loved George, and he was dependent upon her, both physically and emotionally. Naturally, she did all that she could for him.

It is not so clear how George felt about her sacrifice and his own dependence. He seems to have accepted the situation with reasonably good cheer. He was, like his wife, an optimistic, good-natured person, and her love and devotion must have softened any pain he felt in acknowledging his dependence upon her. But George was also both aware of his wife's artistic gifts and proud of them, and it is not clear how he justified in his own mind her sacrifice of her own career to a great extent in order to help him. In fact, of course, his career supported them both financially.

The first few years back in Indianapolis were especially difficult ones for the Messes. George was weak and anemic; on more than one occasion, Evelynne recalls, he fainted in public. Evelynne took a course in home nursing when she realized that he was not getting better, and she found the training continuously useful.

Despite his illness George produced a large number of etchings during the fall and winter of 1940-1941, and he had a burst of creativity in March, 1941, when he created eight new etchings, several of them miniatures. Several 1940 works—*Neighbors*, *Tangled Branches*, *Winter in the Hills*, and *Wishing Gate in Winter*, along with *Ever So Humble* (1937)—won the Hoosier Salon's Cunningham Prize for etchings in 1941. The same year George also exhibited an oil painting, *Around the Hill Top*, at the Indiana Artists' Club, as he was to do annually for many more years. In fact, 1941 was to be George's last year as a prolific etcher. While many of his finest aquatints were etched in the ensuing years, etching, as noted above, thereafter ceased to be the primary focus of George's interest. He returned to painting.

Why did George turn away from the medium that had brought him so much attention and success? Evelynne offers several explanations. For one thing etchings are harder to prepare than paintings. The technique is confining and time-consuming. Etching was wearing George out. Moreover, Evelynne points out, the greatest national recognition was given to painters—not etchers. The best-known artists were most often painters; the biggest, most pretigious shows were painting exhibits. George's first love was painting, and he had never stopped painting—even during the busiest years with the Esquire company. And painting could be done in stages; George could work for as long as his energy lasted and then rest, with no harm to the painting.

But while George's output as an etcher dwindled to two or three a year for most years after 1942, the quality of those prints was such that they continued to be accepted for major exhibits and to win prizes for the rest of his life. George Jo Mess prints appeared annually (with few exceptions) at the Society of American Graphic Artists exhibits in New York, the Library of Congress exhibits in Washington, the Chicago Society of Etchers, and the Ohio Society of Printmakers in Dayton.

In the winter of 1941-1942 the Messes bought a forty-acre farm a few miles east of Nashville, Indiana. The John Followell farm, as it was known, was bordered on the south by Clay Lick Creek and was a fine example of Brown County terrain: "hills and dales and creeks and valleys," Evelynne recalls. There were a number of small outbuildings on the property along with a good-sized barn ("a poor sad-looking thing, with no windows") and a modest dwelling house they described humorously as "three rooms and a path." There was no plumbing and no running water. It was precisely the kind of rustic, simple old farm that had appealed so strongly to George Mess as a subject for his work.

Now, however, he would learn to live the life he portrayed so often in his art.

Brown County was already a well-established center for artists long before the Messes came in 1942. "Discovered" by artists in the years after the turn of the century, the Nashville area had attracted both T. C. Steele and the Wisconsin painter Adolph Shulz as residents by 1908. Shulz estimated that there were twenty-five artists working in Brown County in the summer of 1908, nearly all of them living in a hotel run by local art enthusiasts. By 1926 there was a sufficiently large number of Nashville area artists to prompt the opening of an art gallery and the founding of the Brown County Art Association.[1]

Evelynne had known Brown County since her childhood experiences at summer camp there, and she and George had frequently driven down on weekends for a day's sketching since the late 1920s. Some of George's most successful aquatint etchings had been Brown County scenes from the beginning of his career as an etcher: *Wishing Gate* and *The Hitching Post*, for example. And, as Evelynne points out, George Jo Mess was a *landscape* painter. Brown County had some of the most striking landscapes around. Its hilly isolation had preserved much of its natural world from exploitation as intensively farmed land.

Besides the artistic attractions of Brown County, Evelynne and George were drawn to country life as a potential aid to George's health. The farm kept them outdoors a great deal. While they never actually farmed their land, they did keep an acre of vegetable and flower gardens. Although they generally only stayed for weekends, the outdoor life was good for George.

The early 1940s were recuperative years for George. He and Evelynne had sold their share of the engraving company after some disagreements with the other owners (including George's brother Gordon) over distribution of profits, having realized much less from their investment than they had expected. Their primary income source was free-lancing, especially illustrating books. George illustrated a number of textbooks and the Bible for the publishing companies in Chicago, but his best-

George Jo Mess, *The Handy Pump*, 1943, aquatint

Evelynne Mess, *Holiday in the Country*, 1948, aquatint

known assignment was Jeannette Covert Nolan's *Hoosier City, the Story of Indianapolis*, published in 1943. Because the publisher failed to give George a concrete assignment and schedule in advance, he found himself asked to create more than forty illustrations in about a month.[2] For a meticulous worker like George, this must have been a kind of nightmare, especially since he had to do considerable research to illustrate a variety of historical periods. Although George alone was credited as the artist (and the style is recognizably his), it is obvious that he received extensive assistance from Evelynne in turning his sketches into finished pen-and-ink drawings for the book. Together the Messes undertook many such assignments in these years.

In 1942-1943 Evelynne returned for one year to full-time teaching. Substituting for an artist on leave, she greatly enjoyed her year at the Ladywood school, an exclusive college preparatory academy and boarding school for young women.

The artists encountered another turning point in their careers in 1944 when they began a three-year close association with the nationally renowned portrait painter Wayman Adams (1883-1959). Adams, too, was a Hoosier, born in Muncie, and a John Herron student from 1904 to 1908. After studying in Italy with William Merritt Chase, and in Spain with Robert Henri, Adams rose swiftly to prominence through his arresting portraits of Indianapolis subjects Booth Tarkington and Alexander Ernestinoff, the latter work winning a prize at the National Academy of Design exhibit in 1914. By 1926 Adams had been elected a member of the National Academy, and in 1933 he opened his own school in Elizabethtown, New York, where he also lived and painted.[3]

Adams had maintained a studio in Indianapolis from 1911 to the early 1930s, and he was, of course, a very important member of the Indianapolis art community. Evelynne and George had known Adams since their student days in the 1920s, when he was already a well-established painter. Adams had joined the Indiana Society of Printmakers in 1934 at Evelynne's invitation and knew the Messes' work. Early in 1944 he invited

them to spend the summer teaching etching and lithography at Elizabethtown. He offered a salary in addition to the promise of a summer of painting and etching in the Adirondacks.[4]

The prospect of a summer in the country with a change of scenery *and* the opportunity to spend time with Adams and his artist wife Margaret was an appealing one. The setting was comfortable. The Adamses had bought an old mill and outbuildings on the outskirts of the little summer resort town located on the Bouquet River. Together they had created "Mill Village"—with a large studio in the mill, accommodations for students and faculty, a restaurant, and a large and impressive home nearby for themselves.

It was an informal, stimulating summer. The students were serious; the landscape was splendid; the company and entertainments were pleasing. The Adamses were hospitable hosts. As Evelynne recalled later,

> Every day and night brought an interesting and new experience, long to be remembered and cherished. Wayman Adams, his wife Margaret and George and I were constant companions when not teaching. Wayman, as we called him, encouraged informality and use of first names among the students and teachers. Cool evenings were spent around the Adamses' fireplace for discussion on art. George and I had charge of the Graphic Arts Department. The whole ground floor was turned over to us for printmaking. I taught mostly etching and lithography. We took Edmund Brucker—a teacher at Herron—along to be our assistant and monitor of the print department. George taught landscape painting when not busy with printmaking. We also found time to be in one of Adams's portrait painting classes. He and Mrs. Adams would come to our printmaking studio in their spare time and draw on litho stones, and we'd help them make lithographs sometimes in the evenings. We never wasted time, always enjoying our art work.

There was also some time for painting the countryside, and George and Evelynne responded with a burst of productivity. They sold much of what they painted, and Evelynne recalls that it was a profitable summer for them in every way. Certainly when George showed his Adirondacks paintings, the critics were impressed. *Adirondack Solitude* won the Indiana Artists' Club's T. C. Steele prize that fall; *Adirondacks* won a Hoosier Salon prize in January, 1945, and in March his solo exhibit of twenty oils at the Hoosier Gallery in Indianapolis was greeted with praise.[5]

Adams was in the process of detaching himself from the Elizabethtown school when he invited the Messes to join him there in 1944. He and his wife were planning to move to Texas and were looking for someone to take over their school. They proposed that the Messes do this, but George and Evelynne did not want to move to New York. They did, however, return for two more summers of teaching in 1945 and 1946. The summer of 1945 was memorable for the production of a demonstration aquatint by Evelynne that became perhaps her most critically acclaimed etching, *Adirondack Trail*. This work was shown at the National Academy of Design and the Society of American Etchers and was purchased by the Library of Congress for its permanent print collection. "This one took six weeks to complete," Evelynne recalled.

> Each step in the process was done while the students watched me. I just took a part of each class time to work on it—that is why it took so long. I etched eighteen tones (shades of light gray to black) preparatory to hand printing the final proof. If I hadn't accomplished another thing except this etching, I would have been well rewarded.

The summer was also memorable because of the appearance of a long article about George in the June, 1945, issue of *American Artist*. Ernest W. Watson, coeditor of the magazine and author of numerous art instruction textbooks, devoted over six pages to a generously illustrated article on George and his etching technique. With Evelynne acting as secretary, George described the aquatint process and provided examples of his work in preparation for the etching, *The Goat Farm*, including an oil painting, a detailed drawing, the plate itself, and photographs of the open plate process. Watson described George as "one of the most gifted of American Printmakers."[6]

In 1946 after their last summer at the Adams school George and Evelynne spent a week at

Princeton in the fall. George had been commissioned by the Princeton Print Club to create an etching of Stanhope Hall, on the Princeton campus, to be offered as the regular annual membership print of the club.[7] The Messes visited with their friends, the Reverend and Mrs. Elmer Homrighausen, formerly from Indianapolis. The Homrighausens' home on Mercer Street was next door to that of Albert Einstein. The unpretentious and warm Einstein sat for a pencil portrait by Evelynne.

These were flourishing years for the Messes. Both were exhibiting widely and receiving considerable recognition. Two of the aquatints George created in 1945 became part of the Library of Congress' permanent collection; one, *Living Better Without*, won the Joseph Pennel purchase prize for the library's exhibit. George won both the major print prize and a landscape prize at the Hoosier Salon in 1946, and one of his aquatints won the first prize for prints at the California Society of Etchers exhibit the same year. Evelynne's etchings *Country Church* (1946) and *Nature's Lace Work* (1935) won the Hoosier Salon print prize in 1947, while George's paintings *Love* and *Hill Top Pond* won prizes for oils in the same exhibit and in several other shows that year. On the basis of their reputations for outstanding work in these years, they were both invited by the National Academy of Design to show their work without submitting it to a jury in 1946 and 1947.

Both artists mounted shows during these years. In one about sixty of George's aquatints were exhibited at the Dayton (Ohio) Art Institute in 1942. As mentioned earlier, George's Adirondacks paintings were featured in a solo show at the Hoosier Gallery in Indianapolis in March, 1945, and he also mounted solo shows at that gallery in 1951 and 1953. George and Evelynne had several shows together—at Lieber's in November, 1945; the Hoosier Salon Gallery in September, 1947; at Lieber's again in March, 1949; and at the Hoosier Salon Gallery again in February, 1959. And both were invited to exhibit in duo shows with other Indiana artists in the series begun in 1947 at the Herron Art Institute. George Mess and Robert Laurent of

George Jo Mess, *The Goat Farm*, 1944, aquatint

George Jo Mess, *Living Better Without*, 1945, aquatint

George Jo Mess, *Picnic*, 1953, aquatint

George Jo Mess, *Farm House Interior*, 1942, oil

Evelynne Mess, *Family Circle*, 1952, oil

George Jo Mess, *Outing*, 1945, oil

George Jo Mess, *Main Street*, 1947, aquatint

George Jo Mess, *Coffee Time*, 1951, aquatint

George Jo Mess, *Sawmill*, 1949, aquatint

Bloomington inaugurated the series in October; Evelynne and Roy Trobaugh came soon after.[8]

Evelynne received some special recognition in the late 1940s. George was finally feeling better, and this fact was reflected in her work. Buoyed by the reception of *Adirondack Trail* in 1945 and 1946, as it made its way triumphantly around the major print shows, Evelynne's productivity and participation in juried exhibits rose notably. She won the Renee Barnes purchase prize of the Tri-State Print Exhibition in 1946 (the successor of the Indiana Society of Printmakers Annual Exhibit) with *In the Mountains*. As mentioned before, at the 1947 Hoosier Salon she won the prize for the best group of prints. In 1948 her painting *Old Fashioned Bouquet* won second prize in the National Society for Arts and Letters national arts competition in Chicago, and in December of that year she won a purchase prize at the Indiana Print Show. After her duo show with George in March, 1949, Evelynne's *Adirondack Trail* was featured on the cover of the Indianapolis Sunday *Star Magazine*, May 15, 1949, which included a substantial, well-illustrated article about the artist. But the climax of this surge of public recognition was perhaps

George attracts a curious audience while painting on a street in Aurora, Indiana.

the response to her contributions to the Indiana Artists' Club show in Indianapolis in October. Her painting *Committee Women* won the Clowes award and the enthusiastic praise of local critics. Herbert Kenney, Jr., called it "provocative" and "hugely amusing." Lucille Morehouse was prompted to describe Evelynne as "the most original and the most naively creative worker with pictorial design among our younger artists who always have something to say." Morehouse's advice to Evelynne was to stay in her studio for the next ten years and "paint like fury."[9]

In 1949 George embarked on a career that was to be important to him for the rest of his life. He began to teach art to part-time college students at the then downtown branch of Indiana University. Teaching was not new to George, of course. He had had some five years teaching experience at the Circle Art Academy, and he had taught at the Wayman Adams School for three summers. George was an experienced public speaker; he lectured all over the state from time to time throughout the years, most often delivering a demonstration lecture on aquatint. But the I. U. appointment gave him a permanent base, and his commitment to teaching never flagged. His friend and fellow artist Floyd Hopper recalled that George found teaching an interesting challenge and worked all summer to prepare for his winter classes. He was successful as well as dedicated; his students liked and respected him. In addition to the permanent base at the I. U. branch, George also became a regular instructor (along with Evelynne) for the Indianapolis Art League and occasionally taught summer classes at the Herron Institute.

Evelynne, too, began to undertake regular teaching assignments during the 1950s. One long-term commitment was to the Indianapolis Art League, where she taught for most of two decades. She also supervised classes sponsored by the Indianapolis Art League for patients at Central State Hospital in Indianapolis in 1953, in an effort to provide useful therapy for the mentally ill.[10] She was later to have her own art school in Nashville, Indiana, in the 1960s and 1970s.

The teaching that the Messes undertook in the

1950s was carried on despite recurrences of George's illness in the beginning and ending years of the decade. Ironically, George Mess always *looked* husky and strong. He was over six feet tall and weighed about two hundred pounds. No one other than his doctor and his family knew that George Jo Mess was not as healthy as he looked. He carried increasingly fuller loads of teaching at the I. U. branch as the years went by. In 1953 he was offering freehand drawing and oil painting two long days a week (Mondays and Fridays from 1 P.M. to 10 P.M., with a two-hour dinner break). In the 1960-1961 school year yet another class was added, introduction to drawing, and he was teaching all of the studio art courses offered at the school.

George also managed to paint and etch and play a large role in the art community through this period. He was president of the Indiana Society of Printmakers, 1948-1949, after having organized the tri-state print shows begun in 1944. Both George and Evelynne were officers and active committee members for the Indiana Artists' Club. George was president of the club in 1950-1951, and both Messes frequently served as members of the board of directors and members of the exhibitions committee. They were both also active in the Brown County Art Gallery Association and together mounted a show for the association in 1954 that was described as "the largest and finest show ever presented here." Both frequently acted as judges for art contests. In 1950 they were appointed members of the advisory council for the local chapter of the National Society for Arts and Letters and were subsequently active in the art scholarships program of that organization. Evelynne had resumed her membership in the Indiana Federation of Art Clubs after their return from Chicago and by the early 1950s was taking an active part in the federation's programs; she was chairman of the state convention, for example, in 1952.[11]

After 1950, because her lungs had been injured by overexposure to the nitric acid she used for etching, Evelynne essentially abandoned printmaking for nearly twenty years, but her productivity as a painter increased dramatically. She followed

Morehouse's advice to "paint like fury" as best she could. She created nearly sixty paintings in the decade of the 1950s, and many of them won prizes in Indiana shows (*Cucurbita*, 1952, Hoosier Salon; *In My Studio*, 1956, Holcomb Prize, John Herron Exhibit; *Aquarium*, 1957, Hoosier Salon; *Foot Bridge*, 1957, Indiana Artists' Club; *Calendula Leaves*, 1955, Depauw University Purchase Award; *Field Flowers*, 1958, Hoosier Salon; *Lake Shore*, 1951, Indiana Artists' Club).

George produced about one hundred paintings and thirty aquatints during the 1950s. His prints continued to win places in large national shows—he was virtually always represented in the annual Society of American Graphic Artists exhibit in New York, the Library of Congress exhibit in Washington, and the Society of Etchers show, and his prints won prizes at the latter in 1952 and 1956. In 1950 two of George's aquatints from the Library of Congress collection were selected for the five-month exhibit at the Library: *Indiana: The Sesquicentennial of the Establishment of the Territorial Government*. One of them, *Living Better Without*, was published in the exhibit catalogue. His *Highway No. 7*, 1951—perhaps his most beautifully composed etching—won a prize at the Dallas National Print Competition in 1954 and was exhibited and purchased by the Metropolitan Museum of Art in New York in 1952. He also exhibited there in 1955, and in 1958 ten of his prints were shown in a well-received ten-man show in Washington, D.C., where a local critic praised "fine tonal values as well as pictorial appeal."[12]

While George's aquatints with their traditional subject matter continued to win acclaim, his paintings never received a similar recognition at the national level. As the 1950s wore on, his paintings grew more abstract and his style more experimental. The physical obstacles involved in sending paintings to shows discouraged him rather quickly from mounting a sustained effort to exhibit nationally. While his failure to achieve national recognition as a painter must have rankled and disappointed him, George continued to win the accolades of his Hoosier peers. His paintings regularly won prizes for landscape and composition at the Hoosier Salon (*Paradise Valley*, 1950; *Lake Near Bean Blossom*, 1955; *Winter Patterns*, 1955; *Early Spring Patterns*, 1958) and an eerie *Plant Life in Moonlight*, 1961, won the still life prize in 1962. He also received prizes at the Indiana Artists' Club shows: *Foothills*, 1951; *Full Moon*, 1952; *Fall Bouquet*, 1953; *Wishing Well by Walk*, watercolor, 1955.

George Jo Mess, 1898-1962

In the late 1950s George began to struggle with more frequent occurrences of his illness, which required surgery. Still, he taught his classes and served on committees and continued to paint. In 1960 he created sixteen paintings and four etchings. During these years the Messes were very busy persons. They entertained generously and often in Brown County; their hospitality was famous throughout the community. In addition to produc-

ing regular entries for juried shows, George prepared new work for a joint show with Evelynne at the Hoosier Salon Gallery in February, 1959, and mounted a solo show at the Jewish Community Center in Indianapolis in May, 1960.

In mid-April, 1962, George began to notice that his right hand felt numb and awkward, and a few weeks later he began to experience spasms in his right arm. Up to this time illnesses had not impaired his ability to draw and paint, but this one threatened to remove the greatest joy and meaning from his life. In answer to the question about whether or not George knew he was desperately ill, Evelynne's answer is always the same:

> George was a very innocent person. He was also by nature a complete optimist. Even I could almost believe he would recover—he was such a big, strong-looking man. Finally, the Indianapolis surgeon told me after his last operation that there was no hope of saving him and that he must be told the truth. Sometimes I think even telling him then was a mistake, because from that minute he became a completely changed man—mentally and in spirit. He just gave up.

He kept a brave front for the rest of the world. A woman who worked at the Downtown Center recalled seeing George a few days before his death, and he read her palm.[13] However, at home he was a different man. George's depression was intense, and Evelynne wept inside. Hoping a few days in the country would ease their despair, they drove to Brown County the weekend of June 1-3. But two weeks later George collapsed, unconscious, and he died on June 24, 1962, in Methodist Hospital in Indianapolis, never having regained consciousness. He was six days short of his sixty-fourth birthday.

The tributes were quick in coming. An Indianapolis *Star* editorial by Jameson Campaigne on June 27 reflected that "George Jo Mess was one of the finest artists that Indiana has ever produced. And he was one of our finest art teachers. Essentially a simple and sympathetic man, he not only inspired his students by his talent but also won their affection and deep friendship." An Indianapolis *News* editorial the preceding day described George as "internationally known as an artist with

George Jo Mess, *Covered Well*, 1954, aquatint

George Jo Mess, *Winter Patterns*, 1955, oil

George Jo Mess, *Radiant Autumn*, 1956, oil

George Jo Mess, *Monument Circle*, 1958, oil

a gift for capturing the rural and pioneer Hoosier scene." The Brown County Art Gallery Association published "A Loving Tribute to George Jo Mess" on June 28:

Not one of his associates in the Brown County Art Gallery Association needs to be reminded of the unfailing kindness, helpfulness, and tolerance of this good friend. He said it all himself, and often without words . . . the many years of his devotion to the arts brought him prestige, but he seemed unaware of it. . . . We never knew him to discourage another painter, though there must have been times when he was sorely tempted. He would give an opinion, always constructive, and stop, having given an idea that might have far-reaching results. He wanted to help.

One student wrote to Evelynne her memories of George as a teacher:

He would talk of music and art and even drama and he very cleverly wove the web of all the arts into one. He taught us a new way of art as a way of life really. Always saying we must be so sincere, always paint from the heart, above *all things* we must paint from the heart.

Like everyone else, the student commented with obvious affection and respect on George's warmth and generosity of spirit. "George gave of himself, his spirit and soul went out and incorporated each one of us. We all loved him so and I believe that is why."[14]

Notes

1. Adolph R. Shulz, "The Story of the Brown County Art Colony," *Indiana Magazine of History*, XXXI (1935), 282-86.

2. Indianapolis *Star*, October 31, 1943.

3. John Herron Art Museum, *Wayman Adams, N.A. 1883-1959: Memorial Exhibition of Paintings December 6-December 27, 1959* (Indianapolis, 1959); Indianapolis *News*, May 7, 1926; Indianapolis *Star Magazine*, September 1, 1957.

4. Indianapolis *Star*, June 25, 1944; Nashville *News*, May 13, 1944.

5. Indianapolis *News*, October 23, 1944; Indianapolis *Star*, March 11, 1945.

6. Ernest Watson, "A Hoosier Artist: George Jo Mess," an *American Artist* IX (June, 1945), 14.

7. *Daily Princetonian*, May 13, 1947.

8. Dayton (Ohio) *Journal-Herald*, April 19, 1942; Indianapolis *Star*, October 21, 1951; October 11, 1953; September 28, 1947; March 6, 1949; October 19, 1947; March 21, 1948; clippings in EMD scrapbook, pp. 71 and 83.

9. Indianapolis *News*, October 12, 1949; Indianapolis *Star*, October 14, 1949.

10. Indianapolis *Star*, April 12, 1953.

11. Clippings in EMD scrapbook, pp. 73, 102; Indianapolis *Star*, March 17, 1950; Indianapolis *News*, April 26, November 29, 1952.

12. Cleveland *Plain Dealer*, March 21, 1954; Washington *Star*, August 31, 1958.

13. Jeannette Matthew interview, May, 1984.

14. Clipping in GJM scrapbook, p. 46; Dorothy Dahlstrom to Evelynne Mess, n.d. (circa March, 1963).

George Jo Mess, *Highway No. Seven*, 1951, aquatint

George Jo Mess, *Stanhope Hall*, 1946, aquatint

Evelynne Mess Daily, *Pot-Belly Stove*, 1973, lithograph

Chapter 6

Evelynne Mess Daily

"Marriage," says Evelynne, "is wonderful if the persons involved are truly partners, especially if they work together in a field they both love, as George and I did. We shared everything we did in art and complemented each other. I was lost when he died."

Until that moment, their work together had enabled Evelynne to ignore her own despair at thoughts of losing her partner. Now reality, as she reread the obituaries and answered letters of sympathy, bore down upon her.

For a while as Evelynne read the kind words she could think of nothing else but her loss and loneliness. Deep depression became an unwelcomed guest, threatening to remain with her forever. Painting and etching seemed inconceivable to her. Why attempt to create anything without George to share it?

Eventually her lifelong work habits and the blessing of her inherently optimistic view came to her rescue. She resumed teaching at the Art League and the South Side Art League. At the same time she began to catalogue George's works.

For most of the first year after George's death Evelynne prepared for a memorial exhibit of his works at the request of Wilbur Peat, director of the John Herron Institute. She worked with Peat to assemble a representative selection of the best of George's paintings and etchings, sometimes limited by what they could persuade owners to lend to the museum for the exhibit. Together they chose twenty-nine of George's paintings—beginning with the pre-Fontainebleau *Snow Covered City* (1925) and ending with *Sand Slopes* (1961). Most of those selected were from his mature works as a painter in the last decade of his life, many of them abstract and exploring a wide range of techniques.

Clearly the landscape that preoccupied the mature George Mess was not Brown County—it was the "landscape" of his imagination. The aquatints selected for the show were a more traditional lot, as to be expected. They were fairly evenly distributed over his years as an etcher, beginning with *Southern Oak* (1936) and ending with *Do Come Around* and *In Full Moon* from 1957. Assembling the work and searching through her profusion of records to date the pieces was an enormous task, but it was a healing one as well.

This exhibition ran from March 31 to April 21, 1963, and attracted considerable public notice. One Indianapolis commentator observed that Mess's work "is distinctive for superb tonal arrangements and strong compositions." There were other memorial programs and exhibits to follow—all calling upon Evelynne's skills as an organizer of shows. The Indiana Chapter of the National Society of Arts and Letters (1963), the Indianapolis Art League (1964), the Indiana University-Purdue University Downtown Center (1966), and the Sheldon Swope Galleries in Terre Haute (1966) all honored George with programs and/or exhibits.[1]

With the coming of spring, Evelynne's thoughts turned to Brown County. She and George had long planned to convert their barn into a studio in order to hold a full-time summer school—a smaller Indiana version of Wayman Adams's Milltown. George, interested in remodeling, had already arranged to have the smaller barn turned into a guesthouse, in which was installed a large window he picked up from a Nashville grocer. Before his death in 1962, George and Evelynne had the large barn's foundation raised and part of a cement floor poured. Evelynne now decided to go on with the plan. She had the floor completed, interior walls washed, and windows added to the old doors and walls. Some of the stall partitions were removed, leaving areas large enough for potters, printmakers, painters, and other craftsmen to work in.[2]

The school's original name was apparently Brown County Art Studios. Evelynne, alone, taught the first summer. By the second season she had brought in potter Harry Gillespie to teach ceramics on Saturday mornings. In 1967 the school's name changed and the curriculum was greatly expanded—so much so that Evelynne was describing it as "the new art school in Brown County 'Oxbow Acres.'" The school was open from May until mid-October, and Evelynne had help from craftsman Leonard Kord, who taught art glass and mosaics. During the fall session she was joined by Charles Barnes, director of the Modern Art Center of Brown County, for Tuesday and Wednesday classes. At various times she also offered silk screening and metal enameling in addition to a full range of printmaking, painting, and drawing. There were usually ten to fifteen students in each of the classes. The landscape painters were free to roam over the forty-two acre farm for recreation and in search of subject matter, and each worked at his own pace.[3]

Great emphasis was placed on printmaking. In the first stall on the right of the double-door entrance, its huge wheel dominating that corner of the studio-workshop, was the antique hand-etching press Evelynne had acquired long ago. The stall served not only as the printmaking center but also as a gallery in which to display students' work and, for inspiration, some of the best of Evelynne's and George's prints.

In other stalls were hung drawings and paintings, and the studio scintillated with inspiring examples of ceramics, flower arrangements, jewelry, and colored glass. The aesthetic nature of the surroundings, inside and out, along with Evelynne's dedication and enthusiasm, could only have raised the spirits of all who studied there and confirmed in them a wish to excel in their work.

Beginning in 1964 the old farmhouse, long the weekend retreat for Evelynne and George, served as her abode each year from April til November.

She enjoyed this long break from city living. Gardening continued to occupy many hours. Spring, the woods and meadows singing with new life, and the glorious scarlet and purple and gold of autumn called her outdoors. She lingered in the hills and valleys to record on canvas and in her sketchbook landscapes, weathered buildings, and the flowers and trees and creatures abounding there. By the time winter came, she had gathered rainbows of multitudinous materials to carry back to Indianapolis in her van studio-on-wheels. She used these sketches in paintings she would create when bad weather rendered working outdoors unattractive or inconvenient.

The mid-sixties ushered in a period that would become one of the most productive of Evelynne's life. Now there blossomed on canvas and paper all those enticements of nature she so enjoyed—the wild sweet peas, day lilies, honeysuckle, lady slippers, mushrooms, berries, and meadow grasses and vines; the pine trees, sassafras, wild cherries, maples, red bud and cypress; and the white-tailed deer, raccoons, possums, wild geese, cardinals, meadowlarks, blue jays, and grouse. Between 1963 and 1969, she painted forty-one pictures, nearly all with natural subjects. She exhibited at the Hoosier Salon in 1964, 1965, 1967, 1970, and 1980 and continued to show her paintings regularly in the Brown County Art Association and Indiana Artists' Club shows.

In the winter Evelynne continued to teach for the Indianapolis Art League and became a much sought-after judge for art events, both local and national in scope. She also continued to participate actively in the Indiana Federation of Arts Clubs, with which she had worked for so many years. In August, 1967, Evelynne was asked to be a candidate for president of the organization. "We want someone who is a leader in Art Circles," wrote the chairman of the nominating committee, "whose name means something in the State, a good artist of fine reputation with an honest and sincere approach, and one who will stand up for high ideals in art. We think you are that person."[4] She was elected that fall and served a two-year term. Evelynne had worked for years on program commit-

Evelynne Mess, *Committee Women*, 1949, oil

Evelynne Mess, *In My Studio*, 1956, oil

Evelynne Mess, *Fountain of Youth*, 1948, oil

Evelynne Mess, *Seed Pods*, 1959, oil

tees of the federation, and her leadership was recognized with gratitude during her term as president. It was during her presidency that the annual art appreciation course was replaced by an annual weekend of supervised painting, a "short course" in painting.

While presiding at the tea table at the opening of the 1968 spring exhibit of the Brown County Art Association, Evelynne looked up to meet the eyes of an old friend and recently bereaved widower, Edward R. Daily. Through common interests, she had been acquainted with the Dailys (Daily was head of the printing department at Eli Lilly and Company), but she had more or less lost touch with them in recent years. She soon was to be back in touch with Ed, however, for he steadily sought her company. As their courtship became serious, the pleasure they enjoyed in shared interests and a similar outlook on life revealed within each a wish to be married. Twelve months after Evelynne poured Daily's tea at the Brown County Art Gallery, she was to begin presiding at the table they would share as man and wife.

Daily had left Indianapolis for Brown County upon his retirement and built a house on Route 135 just north of Nashville. Though Evelynne retained possession of her house and studio on Central Avenue in Indianapolis, she was happy to move into the Brown County residence with her new husband. Now she had three studios in which to work—Daily had seen to it that a room in their house would be reserved for Evelynne's exclusive use—where she could draw and paint at leisure those creatures abounding in the country and the moods of the four seasons. Above all, she had found a person she had grown to love with whom to share her life and world of art.

"Ed was a wonderful man," she says.

And we did so many things together—music, theatre, galleries and museums. And we had a nice social life—he liked to be with people. Between us we had many friends. Though he wasn't an artist in the usual sense of the word, he loved and appreciated fine art and all things associated with it. He encouraged me and helped me—literally, at times when he'd make frames, cut mats, assist me in getting ready for exhibits, for instance—said he wanted me to devote myself to my art and my teaching. And he was so practical—could do and fix anything and took care of all those chores, business, everything I had always done that took time away from painting. . . . We were so happy together. . . .

During the next five years, Evelynne's newfound freedom glistened in her life like a precious jewel. She produced nearly forty paintings between 1969 and 1974 and some fourteen prints, mostly lithographs.

Evelynne continued to hold classes at Oxbow Acres every year from May til October, giving each student individual attention. From time to time throughout the existence of the school, other artist-teachers also served on the staff or journeyed to Brown County to give demonstrations, among them Charles Surendorf, John van Bibber, Billie Cothran, Lenora Daily, and Harry Gillespie. The art school attracted students from all over the state until Evelynne reluctantly closed the doors and sold the entire property in 1980.

Her delight with the progress of her school was exceeded only by the satisfaction she realized through her personal accomplishments. During those highly productive years following 1963, the artist submitted works to a number of exhibitions. A select group of Indiana artists, "The Twenty," of which she was a member, exhibited in 1964 her two prize winners, *Brown County Squashes* and *Leaves*. Another award winner, the oil, *In My Studio*, was shown in the 1966 Ball State University exhibition, "One Hundred Years of American Art."

Nineteen sixty-six marked the sesquicentennial of Indiana statehood. The Indiana chapter of the American Society of Arts and Letters initiated a program to pay tribute to the arts and artists of the state. Organized by a dedicated committee of Indianapolis citizens co-chaired by Dorothy Helmer and John Walsh, the program synchronized for nine golden days in October an alliance of the visual arts, drama and literature, music and dance in exhibitions and performances throughout the city. During this celebration the following Evelynne Mess contributions took blue ribbons: *Magic Touch of Winter* and *Leaves* (both oils), *Holiday in* the *Country* and *Branching Willow* (aquatint etchings), and *Abstract* (watercolor). She also won recognition for the best display at University Park with an arrangement on a three-panel screen (created by Ed Daily) of fifteen paintings and etchings placed imaginatively around her large oil, *Fountain of Youth*, a University Park scene she had painted in 1948 for her living room wall.

A shining high point of her life was her 1970 solo exhibition at the Brown County Art Gallery. Twenty-five of her works, both paintings and etchings, were shown with great success. Joanne Couch, staff writer for the Bloomington *Tribune*, praised her in an article that included reproductions of four paintings, *Kitchen Still Life, Butterfly Plant and Seed Pods, Haven for Wildlife*, and *Summertime*. Wrote Couch,[5]

> Evelynne Mess Daily's pictures have brought her fame and a continuing source of pleasure for more than fifty years. . . . She has been exhibiting her work in national and international exhibitions since 1934, and she feels very satisfied to be having a solo show in her own back yard with her many friends near enough to see her work. . . . Painting for Mrs. Daily has not been just for the pleasure of sharing a talent with the people, but for fulfilling a need within herself. . . .

The Brown County Art Guild Association awarded her painting *Seed Pods* a special citation at its supporting members exhibition.

After a nearly twenty-year hiatus in her career as a printmaker due to her acid-damaged lungs, Evelynne took up lithography with Ed Daily's encouragement. Though, like etching, lithography is a demanding art, the process does not require the utilization of an acid bath in preparation for printing. Rather, the image to be reproduced is drawn with a crayon, such as Korn's lithograph pencil, usually on a specially prepared plate or stone, chemically treated, then printed. Evelynne created the following lithographs in the early 1970s: *Parasol Mushrooms, Passion Flower, Mother and Babes, Who–o–s Who—The Great Horned Owl, Pot-Belly Stove, Evelynne's Country Kitchen*, and *Indiana Limestone Quarry*, as well as new versions of earlier prints, *Toadstools, Boat House*, and *Happy Frogs*.

Although Evelynne essentially had to abandon her own etching, she persevered in teaching the subject and in doing so produced several noteworthy etchings and aquatint-etchings in the late 1960s and 1970s: *Sans End, Deserted Log Cabins*, and *Praying Mantis*.

Evelynne's most renowned pupil was George, of course. But many Indiana artists whose art has brought them acclaim learned their technique from her. Wilbur Meese, the Messes' student and helper for one, eventually became art director at Eli Lilly and Company. Another successful artist who learned etching from Evelynne and George is the Brown County artist Kenneth Reeves. Helping and encouraging artists, especially young promising ones, has remained one of the compelling motivations of Evelynne's life. Her dedication has not gone unnoticed or unappreciated by art organizations of the state. In 1978 the Indiana Federation of Art Clubs led the way for several groups by awarding her a certificate that reads in part, "In appreciation of service for maintaining the highest and best standards as an Indiana artist and art teacher. . . ."

Not surprisingly, Evelynne has been asked frequently to judge art shows, and she has seldom refused these requests. Although she and George had judged art shows occasionally, not until after his death did she take up that segment of her career in earnest.

Invited to speak at the Swope Art Gallery in Terre Haute, she expounded her views on "Judging Art." Her talk was a good practical introduction to the study of composition, and enlightening to those who have wondered what standards an art judge applies in choosing prizewinning works at an exhibition. "Notice the lines," she said,

> if a landscape is divided so that the horizon is in the center, most likely the arrangement will appear monotonous. But notice the lines moving through space and the direction they take. . . . Lines not only help to give shape to objects, but they lead us into the picture—if properly conceived. . . . Thought of in this light, lines may be called reading aids in the sense that we read into a painting its visual content.

Evelynne also stressed the importance of color craftsmanship or technique and originality as factors to consider in evaluating a painting. It was clear that Evelynne was describing her techniques for creating her own work. Like many another artist she found it difficult to analyze the emotional content of a painting.

> The other side is purely aesthetic and has to do with feeling and emotion. . . . I will not attempt to verbalize on that aspect to any extent but will say that an artist doesn't just paint what he sees. He paints what he feels, using his hands, his head, his heart. . . .

Ed Daily died suddenly in February, 1974, after only five years of their sharing a rare, well-nigh perfect relationship. Again Evelynne was deeply saddened, but again, strengthened by her forward-looking view and creative spirit, she refused to give in to the devastation this second loss might have wrought. She moved back to Indianapolis and continued her same routine of living and working in her Central Avenue studio during the rest of the winter. Then with the coming of April and the blooming of violets and forsythia and redbud in Brown County's meadows and woods, she re-

Oxbow Acres, 1967

turned to Oxbow Acres to paint and teach, nourished and healed by the rejuvenating beauty of nature and the joy of sharing her talents and knowledge with her students. This pattern continued until 1980, when Evelynne, then in her mid-seventies, sold the farm and retired from regular teaching to her full-time home in Indianapolis.

Evelynne has continued to be an active member of organizations to promote art. She served as a director of the Indiana Artists' Club in the late 1970s and hosted the annual Indiana Federation of Art Clubs painting weekend in 1978. When Wilbur Meese formed the new Water Color Society of Indiana in the early 1980s, he recruited Evelynne to be an officer.

She also continues to be an active painter and printmaker. Since 1975 she has created more than fifty paintings and six prints, a record of productivity that rivals her earlier years. She has continued to exhibit at the Hoosier Salon, the Indiana Artists' Club, the Brown County Art Association, and in a variety of other shows around the state. Her lithograph *Indiana Limestone Quarry* (1974) won an IAC purchase award in 1975; *Old Town* (1978), a watercolor, was exhibited in the forty-second National Exhibit of Painting of the Butler Institute of American Painting in Youngstown, Ohio; and *Lakeside Barn* (1980) won an honorable mention in the annual art show sponsored by the National League of American Penwomen.

Evelynne's work also appeared in several duo shows along with George's in the past decade. Close to home, at the Brown County Art Gallery Association, their work was exhibited for most of May, 1977. On the east coast their work was discovered by June and Norman Kraeft of Bethlehem, Connecticut, owners of the June 1 Gallery, who exhibited forty-six of George's aquatints and twenty-one of Evelynne's intaglio prints at a major two-month-long exhibition, November and December, 1978 (with a three-day preview in Bethesda, Maryland, for the gallery's District of Columbia patrons). The gallery continues to handle the Mess-Daily prints. Most recently, George and Evelynne's work was exhibited for more than two months (January 25-March 30, 1981) in the

Evelynne Mess Daily, *Who-o-s Who—The Great Horned Owl*, 1972, lithograph

Evelynne Mess Daily, *Indiana Limestone Quarry*, 1975, oil

Evelynne Mess Daily, *Lakeside Barn*, 1980, oil

Evelynne Mess Daily, *Down on the Farm*, 1980, oil

Evelynne Mess Daily, *Old Homestead*, 1981, watercolor

downtown gallery of the Indianapolis Museum of Art. This duo show consisted entirely of works from the museum's permanent collections. Earlier, in January, 1980, Evelynne's *Adirondack Trail* was featured in another IMA exhibit, "Recent Accessions," along with prints by Durer and Delacroix.[6]

In addition to this regular activity of painting and exhibiting, Evelynne has begun to receive the honors that accrue to successful veterans of many years of achievement. The Indiana Federation of

Evelynne Mess Daily

Art Clubs gave her a leadership award in 1978, and the Hoosier Salon honored her in 1979 (along with six others) as one of its longest participating artists. As of 1979 she had exhibited in twenty-six Hoosier Salon shows, beginning in 1931. The Indiana Artists' Club made her an honorary member in 1983, and the Indianapolis Art League cited her fifty years of service at their fiftieth anniversary celebration in June, 1984.

"I like to keep up with what's going on," she says. Constantly busy with some project at her desk or in the studio preparing carefully chosen prints and paintings for exhibition, this small dynamo seems indefatigable. When and how does she manage to find time to paint, one wonders?

As a consequence of her gregarious nature and generous spirit, the artist enjoys an active social life with good friends made through her association with the arts. Sharing the company of others exerts a significant and positive force on her creative efforts. She is fond of people—almost as much as she is of art.

* * * * *

When Evelynne Bernloehr reached voting age—twenty-one in those days—the enfranchisement of women had been achieved only four years previously. Though the passage of the Nineteenth Amendment guaranteed woman's elevation from the role of man's subordinate to that of his companion with equal rights, the effect of such legislation hardly became a part of the outlook of Evelynne's generation or the one immediately to follow. The roles both men and women were expected to play during previous centuries could not be changed over night.

The opposing emotions thus created in women a complexity puzzling to most. How could a woman find her identity as a person and still retain the role which she had been assigned by thought, word, and deed throughout her childhood and youth? Supposing she wanted to become a doctor or a lawyer or an athlete or even an artist? How could she participate in any of those professions and remain a "lady"? Women's enfranchisement had not discouraged many men, who felt their authoritarian role threatened, from asking the latter question, implying that liberation is somehow an ugly state which renders women undesirably competitive.

Some women, Evelynne Bernloehr among them, believed so strongly in their own worth that nothing short of chains could prevent their following the path of liberation. Yet, a subtle guilt, a sense that she must, indeed, desire to place her artist husband's works ahead of her own has dominated her life.

Evelynne Mess Daily, *Dr. Mayo's House*, 1982, aquatint

An article clipped from an unidentified journal and found in her file is revealing. "A person's name is a symbol of identity," it begins, then continues,

Yet, what is the first change a woman usually makes upon marriage? . . . The loss of identity that often results from marriage is not merely symbolic; it is all too real. . . . However personally liberated and independent she may feel, a woman using her husband's surname is seen as an extension of him, with her actions attributable to him . . . .

But in the case of Evelynne Bernloehr and George Jo Mess it is fair to ask whose actions are attributable to whom?

Notes

1. Clipping, GJM scrapbook, p. 46; Terre Haute *Star*, May 21, 1966.

2. Betty J. Lane, "Hoosier Artists: Evelynne Mess," in Indianapolis *Star Magazine*, August 27, 1967.

3. Nashville Brown County *Democrat*, August 27, 1964, September 7, 1967; Bloomington *Tribune*, September 1, 1967; EMD scrapbook, pp. 155, 157.

4. Em Flanigan to Evelynne Mess, August 23, 1967.

5. Bloomington *Tribune*, September 27, 1970.

6. Indianapolis *News*, May 4, 1977, January 23, 1981; Bethesda, Maryland, exhibit catalogue *George Jo Mess: Master of Aquatint and Evelynne Mess Daily: Intaglio Prints, November-December, 1978*.

A History of Printmaking in Indiana

by Martin F. Krause

THE HISTORY OF ORIGINAL PRINTMAKING in Indiana extends over a century. This may be one of the best kept secrets in Indiana art. A few names are well known: Gustave Baumann for his color woodcuts of Brown County, L. O. Griffith for his color etchings, Frederick Polley for his etchings and drawings of Indiana monuments, and more recently Garo Antreasian, Rudy Pozzatti, and Misch Kohn. Evelynne Mess Daily and George Jo Mess join the select ranks of dedicated Indiana printmakers whose work attained a national level.

But even the most ardent connoisseur of Indiana art is often surprised to learn that William Forsyth and J. Ottis Adams of the Hoosier Group painters were also frequent etchers; that early Brown County notables Will Vawter and Adolph Shulz were founders of the Brown County Etcher's Club during World War I; and that Wayman Adams was an occasional lithographer, along with the renowned faculty members of the Herron School of Art in Indianapolis, Donald Mattison, David K. Rubins, Henrik Mayer, Edmund Brucker, and many of their early students in the late thirties, including Harry A. Davis and Floyd Hopper. The reputations of these artists were made in painting or sculpture and certainly their major commitments lay in those directions. Printmaking was a diversion for them, practised on occasion, for the fun of it, one presumes. It is rare to find their prints in numbered editions since, for the most part, they seem to have pulled only a handful of proofs with little intention of exhibiting or selling them. They often did not even bother to pencil sign their works, and most prints were relegated to drawers or loose portfolios in their studios. They were, nevertheless, committed to printmaking for at least some moment in their careers. Printmaking does not exist without commitment.

Unlike drawing or watercolor or even painting or sculpture, the success of which depends more on the ability of the artist than on the materials involved in the work, printmaking, even in its simplest forms, requires equal portions of artistic skill, technical knowledge, and specialized equipment.

Etching, as Evelynne Bernloehr had discovered in 1924, depends on the availability of copper or zinc plates, etching needles to inscribe the lines onto the plate through an acid-resistant ground of wax, gum and resin, acid to bite the lines into the plate, and a press with sufficient pressure to force the ink from the bitten lines onto the paper. In Indiana before 1930, these materials were difficult to come by and the knowledge of the process had to be obtained from technical manuals or by word of mouth and patient practice, since printmaking was not offered in a formal way anywhere in the state. Yet of all the forms of printmaking, etching was king and had been since the revival of the art in Europe in the mid-nineteenth century. It is therefore not surprising that when Evelynne decided to become a printmaker in the 1920s, she decided to become an etcher.

While Evelynne Mess, as recounted above, had to struggle to find a way to learn etching in the 1920s and journeyed to France to find a teacher, it is an ironic fact that printmaking existed in Indiana as early as 1880. William Forsyth (1854-1935) in his 1916 *Art in Indiana* certified that etching had been one of the pursuits of the members of the Bohe Club.[1] When in 1880, John Love and James Gookins closed their First Indiana School of Art in Indianapolis, many of the former students, including Forsyth, took over the rooms in the Saks Building formerly occupied by the school. They adopted the name Bohemian Club, shortened to "Bohe" to accommodate the limited space on their door, and continued their study of art. Evenings devoted to etching were among the artistic and social activities practiced by club members. The etchings were an aspect of their sketching forays into the countryside. Forsyth said that these were the first etchings made in Indiana.[2] Forsyth's recollection is supported by the existence of a few scratchy impressionistic, etched landscapes by Bohe members Forsyth, Fred A. Hetherington (1859-1931), and Thomas E. Hibben (1860-1915) dating from 1880. Hibben became the first sketch artist for the Indianapolis *News* as well as a major collector of European graphics. Hetherington became the head of a structural iron firm, while Forsyth, following study in Munich, became one of the most respected Indiana landscape painters. Forsyth also maintained a long, if intermittant, devotion to etching. After he returned to Indiana from Germany he joined another Munich-trained painter, J. Ottis Adams (1851-1927), in establishing an art school in Muncie. Etching was listed in the first course catalogue of 1889-1890, along with the more customary disciplines of drawing and painting. Either Forsyth or Adams could have taught etching, since Adams also worked occasionally in this medium. By the time of his death in 1927, examples of his etchings lined the wall of the stairway in his studio in Brookville.[3]

The Muncie school folded in 1892, and Forsyth returned to Indianapolis where, in 1905, he joined the staff of the newly opened John Herron Art Institute as a drawing instructor. He considered taking up etching again in 1911[4] and did produce a few small landscapes over the next two years of which he pulled a few proofs for friends such as Thomas Hibben. Even if he was too occupied with painting to give more than a passing moment to his etching, Forsyth was a staunch defender of the art.[5] On November 9, 1913, he delivered an etching demonstration and lecture at Herron. His remarks were quoted in the Indianapolis *Star* the following day:

> They call etching one of the minor arts, but I don't see anything minor about it, unless one judges from

the small fry. It means genius of the highest type. It not only has line but the vivid suggestion of color.

Though Forsyth gave little further attention to his etchings, the growing art colony in Brown County counted some of the country's finest printmakers among its members.

Forsyth maintained in an interview with the Indianapolis *Star* on May 24, 1931, that Thomas Hibben and Fred Hetherington had been the first artists to discover the rustic and isolated beauties of Brown County during the course of one of their sketching excursions in their Bohe Club days. Hetherington eventually bought a cabin north of Nashville in 1909 and spent part of every year there. James Whitcomb Riley's favorite illustrator, Will Vawter (1871-1941), and landscape painter Adolph Shulz (1869-1963) settled in Nashville in 1908, following the lead of T. C. Steele, who had purchased the land for his House of the Singing Winds in 1907. Shulz recalled that Brown County was endowed with "purple haze, constant changing color, vivid blue sky, inexpensive living and all the things which the artist loves."[6] Many Chicago artists were drawn to the county because it preserved the last vestiges of a pioneer life-style that had disappeared almost everywhere else in the country. Nashville was isolated in the hills and six miles from the nearest rail link at Helmsburg, yet it was not a difficult commute from Chicago.[7] By 1909 there were twenty-five artists working part of the year in Brown County and one of them was the printmaker Gustave Baumann (1881-1971).

Baumann had been producing woodblock prints for four years before his arrival in Nashville in 1909, but his early national reputation rested on the color woodblock prints he created in Brown County. In 1910 Baumann issued a portfolio of twelve three-color woodcuts entitled "In the Hills o' Brown." He accurately depicted the colorful life in and around Nashville with views of the *Rug Weaver*, the *Wagon Shop*, and Allison's *Print Shop*, where the weekly *Brown County Democrat* was published. Baumann had printed the portfolio in this shop on the old Washington hand press (known locally as "the muscle developer") when it was not in use for the newspaper. By 1913 Baumann had purchased a studio overlooking Nashville and was spending most of the year there. His color woodcuts, requiring up to seven blocks for each of the seven colors in a given image, were exhibited nationally and earned him a gold medal for printmaking at the prestigious Panama-Pacific International Exposition in San Francisco in 1915. Two years later Baumann left Nashville, selling his press to Brown County photographer Frank Hohenberger. He went first to Provincetown, Massachusetts, and Wyoming, New York, before heading west for Taos and Santa Fe, New Mexico, where he settled for good in 1918.

Two other Brown County artists were honored for their printmaking at the Panama-Pacific. L. O. Griffith (1875-1956) was a bronze medalist for his color etchings, and Charles Dahlgreen (1864-1955) was honorably mentioned for his line etchings. Like Baumann, Griffith and Dahlgreen were based in Chicago, and both were founding members of the Chicago Society of Etchers in 1910. Griffith had visited Brown County in March, 1907, and he soon became an annual visitor. His specialty was three-color etching, a difficult medium he had perfected about 1910 while working in a Chicago engraving house. In 1922 Griffith decided to settle permanently in Nashville and converted a creamery into a studio, complete with etching press.[8]

Dahlgreen was a seasonal visitor to the art colony by 1918. By 1920 he also had a press there, according to Indianapolis etcher Frederick Polley, who witnessed an inking and printing demonstration by Dahlgreen at that time.[9] Twelve of Dahlgreen's Brown County etchings and fifteen of his paintings were seen in Indianapolis in a one-man show in September, 1923.

Dahlgreen may also have had a hand in the founding of the Brown County Etcher's Club in 1918. The club was located in Will Vawter's Nashville studio above Tilton's corner grocery. According to the Indianapolis *News* of June 7, 1919, the club had a few members and was equipped with the neccessities of etching: a cast-iron cannon stove, table, cheese-cloth for plate-wiping, cans of brown and black printing inks, various etching tools, and a regulation copper plate etching press, "the pride

of Will Vawter's existence." Only Vawter and Adolph Shulz are mentioned as members, and several examples of their Brown County landscape etchings exist in the collection of the Indianapolis Museum of Art. They are dated 1918 and 1919 and are printed on Strathmore Japan paper. In the same collection is a proof of a landscape by Charles Dahlgreen dedicated in March, 1918, "out of friendship" to Adolph Shulz. This etching, also printed on Strathmore Japan, strongly suggests Dahlgreen's affiliation with the club. The Brown County Etcher's Club disappears from the record in 1920, but by 1930 there were enough etchers working in Brown County to justify a catalogue of their work. The publication reproduces thirty-nine etchings by members of the Brown County Art Gallery Association which were for sale at the Artists' Shop in Nashville. Some of Vawter's 1919 etchings were included, as were prints by Griffith and Dahlgreen. The catalogue also features etchings and drypoints by Chicagoans Frank Raymond (b. 1881) and Oscar B. Erickson (b. 1883) and Indianapolis etcher Frederick Polley (1875-1957).

In the capital city, printmakers were not nearly as prevalent or organized. For the first third of this century the only professional printmaker was Frederick Polley, and even he supplemented his income by teaching and providing pencil drawings to the *Sunday Star* once a week. Polley was born in Union City and was trained as a commercial printer. He went to Washington, D.C., around the turn of the century as a government topographer. He was impressed by the major collection of Whistler etchings in the Library of Congress and decided to study the arts of lithography and etching at the Corcoran School of Art. Polley returned to Indianapolis and in 1914 delivered a lecture and demonstration of lithography at the Herron Art Institute. The following year he was hired to teach drawing and design at Manual Training School and, in 1916, transferred to Arsenal Technical School to teach commercial art. Polley also began to produce individual etchings of the prominent architectural monuments of Indianapolis, and over the course of his career, these became the most recognizable aspect of his work. Polley's line work was so popular locally that he converted the attic of his home at

371 S. Emerson in Irvington into an etching studio by 1921. He began exhibiting nationally with the Chicago and American Society of Etchers in 1924. In 1932 Polley was named head of the Graphic Arts Department at Arsenal and added etching and lithography to the curriculum of commercial art, printing, printing design, and advertising layout. To my knowledge, the courses in printmaking offered at Arsenal High School in 1932 were the first of their kind in the state.

Commercial printing had been taught at Arsenal from the inception of the school in 1913, and fine art printmaking must have seemed a logical extension to members of the art faculty. The necessary equipment was at hand, and several of the instructors were creating their own etchings and lithographs by the early thirties. Robert C. Craig, born in Jefferson County and for many years the head of the Arsenal art department, produced fine lithographs, frequently of New England coastal scenes. Edmund Schildknecht (b. 1899) came to Indianapolis from Chicago and was a member of the Arsenal staff from 1931 to 1964. He too was a lithographer and etcher. Walter H. McBride (b. 1905), a 1928 Herron graduate and teacher of design at Arsenal and Herron, created woodcuts and etchings. In 1933 McBride was named director of the Fort Wayne Art School.

Although, as noted above, printmaking was not taught at Herron at that period, many of the museum's personnel were print-minded. The first Curator of Prints and Drawings, Alfred Mansfield Brooks, was hired in 1910. The Harvard-educated Brooks divided his time over the next decade between his curatorship and teaching art history at Indiana University. He was a noted authority on prints and authored *From Holbein to Whistler, Notes on Drawing and Engraving* in 1920. The museum director who served from 1914 to 1922 was Harold Haven Brown (1869-1932), a fine woodcut artist who exhibited this talent in a one-man show at Herron in August, 1923. His successor, J. Arthur MacLean, was an Oriental specialist, but he encouraged his assistant director, Dorothy Blair, to establish a Print Room in the museum and to organize a print class in late 1923. In January,

1924, Blair instituted a series of seven weekly lectures on "The Appreciation of Engravings and Etchings." One of the meetings was devoted to an etching demonstration by Polley. He prepared a copper plate featuring flying geese in the manner of the popular Boston etcher Frank Benson. The twenty members of the class were invited to contribute several lines to the plate before it was printed, and one of the members who did so was Evelynne Bernloehr. This 1924 demonstration was her first practical exposure to the art of etching.

The following year, Blair again offered the print class, consecrating this session to "Wood-cuts and Wood-Engravings." Gustave Baumann, who had maintained his Indiana ties after leaving for the Southwest, sent a set of six wood blocks from Santa Fe. The blocks had been used in his old Brown County print, *The Landmark*, one for each of the six colors in the print. He also sent progressive proofs to demonstrate how each block would appear if singly printed on paper and in progressive combinations, building toward the finished image. One of the meetings of the class was turned over to Blanche Stillson (1890-1977), an instructor at the Herron School of Art, who gave a practicum on linocut printing. Stillson had been interested in that art for several years.

In 1926 Blair's lectures dealt with "The History and Development of Lithography," and the class prepared a demonstration lithograph under the supervision of Earle Wayne Bott (1894-1964) and in conjunction with the Stafford Engraving Company.

Both MacLean and Blair left the museum for other positions in December, 1926, but the tradition of printmaking stayed strong. Stillson remained on the faculty and Paintings Curator Anna Hasselman (1876-1966) was an accomplished etcher and woodcut artist. MacLean was followed in 1929 by Wilbur David Peat (1898-1966), who guided the museum for the next thirty-six years. Peat also dabbled in woodcuts.

One of Peat's early decisions was to provide a forum for Indiana artists, and in December, 1932, he inaugurated a series of one-man exhibitions of deserving Indiana artists. Over the next two years, three printmakers were recognized with two-week shows at the museum: Frederick Polley showed recent etchings and drypoints at Herron in January, 1933; Loreen Wingerd [DeWaard] (b. 1902), a teacher in the Indianapolis school system, exhibited her refined, floral woodcuts; and Evelynne Mess exhibited twenty-nine of her French and Indiana etchings and drypoints the last two weeks of February, 1934. By that time Evelynne had already instituted a broader outlet for the printmakers of Indiana.

At the time, Evelynne Mess was Exhibitions Chairman for the Woman's Department Club of Indianapolis. She conceived of the first exhibition devoted solely to Indiana printmakers. The Woman's Department Club Gallery at 17th and Meridian had often shown Indiana art, but rarely prints.[10] Evelynne invited prints by active Indiana artists or by artists with a clear Indiana connection. Since the community of printmakers was fairly closed, she had little trouble attracting the best of a restricted number of practitioners.

Eighteen printmakers submitted twenty-eight prints for this group showing in January, 1934. Evelynne contributed two of her own etchings; Frederick Polley was represented by two drypoints. Will Vawter and L. O. Griffith sent etchings from Nashville. The Herron staff was represented with woodcuts by Wilbur Peat and Blanche Stillson and with etchings by Anna Hasselman and Earle Wayne Bott. Evelynne also secured the participation of two nationally recognized artists who had maintained their Indiana connections: Wayman Adams and Howard Leigh.

Adams (1883-1959), the noted portraitist, was a Muncie native and Herron graduate. He sent a lithograph from New York. Though he had only recently become interested in lithography, he had already been recognized for his work in this direction at the Art Institute of Chicago's pioneering Second Annual International Exhibition of Lithography and Woodcuts in 1930.

Howard Leigh (1896-1981), born in Kentucky but a longtime resident of Spiceland, Indiana, was an internationally recognized lithographer. Fol-

lowing his graduation from Earlham College in 1918, Leigh went to France to study art at the École des Beaux-Arts in Paris. His first lithographs, a series of twenty-four scenes depicting the devastation of World War I on the French countryside, were a great success in exhibitions in Paris, New York, Chicago, and Indianapolis in 1920-1921. Leigh spent the next decade traveling through Europe, producing black and white lithographs of the picturesque architecture of France, Italy, Germany, and Spain, though he frequently returned to Spiceland in the summer. His work won an honorable mention at the Paris Salon of 1927, and he submitted three of his European lithographs to the Woman's Department Club exhibition: *View of the Cathedral at Ronda, Spain, Moorish Bridge*, and *Arch of Septimus in Rome*. Leigh taught at Earlham briefly in the early thirties before leaving finally for Mexico in 1937.

Carolyn Bradley (1898-1954), a Richmond native residing in Columbus, Ohio, and C. R. Zimmer of Dayton were the other out-of-state participants in the print exhibition.

William Forsyth's daughter, Constance (b. 1903), exhibited two drypoints. She undoubtedly had learned the rudiments of etching from her father and had sharpened her skills while on a scholarship from the Herron Art Institute to the Pennsylvania Academy of the Fine Arts in 1929. Her etchings debuted locally at the Woman's Department Club in 1931. She had also recently completed a course of study in lithography under Boardman Robinson at the Broadmoor Art Academy in Colorado Springs.

The other Indianapolis participants were Paul Shideler (1888-1962), a newspaperman by trade who contributed an etching and an aquatint, Loreen Wingerd, Bird Baldwin, and Robert Selby. Joseph Weiland of Anderson rounded out the exhibition.

The favorable reception of the show encouraged the notion of a more permanent association. Evelynne Mess invited Frederick Polley, Paul Shideler, Constance Forsyth, and Loreen Wingerd to her home on the evening of January 8, 1934, for the purpose of founding an Indiana print club. The proposal was adopted, the name Indiana Society of Printmakers was selected, and officers were nominated. Polley was elected president, Forsyth, vice-president, Mess, secretary-treasurer, Shideler, chairman of the admissions committee, and Wingerd, chairman of the exhibition committee. It was decided to restrict membership to twenty-five professional, practicing craftsmen. A prospectus was printed and sent to forty prospective members whose names Evelynne had culled from the annual *Who's Who in American Art*. The printed circular outlined the Society's objectives:

> To create a forum for the exchange of ideals in the artistic craft of print-making.
>
> To mutually inspire and intelligently encourage its members to produce the highest type of artistic prints.
>
> To foster and encourage the love for the work of the print-makers art in the public mind within the borders of our own state.
>
> To develop an earnest appreciation and intellectual pleasure in the collection and possession of fine prints.
>
> To place before the public worthy examples of the fine prints in the form of exhibitions by its members.

With considerable enthusiasm, twenty-five members joined the society within weeks. The first Members' Exhibit of the Indiana Society of Printmakers was set for May 28 to June 9, 1934, at the H. Lieber Company in Indianapolis.

Eleven of the new members had participated in the Woman's Department Club exhibition. Only Bradley, Baldwin, Bott, Leigh, Selby, Peat, and Vawter did not join. In their places and rounding out the twenty-five were some of the most respected printmakers from around the country. Among them were Chester Leich (b. 1889), originally of Evansville and residing in Leonia, New Jersey, a member of the Chicago Society of Etchers; J. H. Euston of Gary, a well-known painter and etcher of the Dunes; LeRoy D. Sauer (1894-1959) of Dayton, founder of the Dayton Society of Etchers in 1921 and the Ohio Printmakers in 1928;

Lee Sturges of Elmhurst, Illinois, the president of the Chicago Society of Etchers; Harry LeRoy Taskey (1892-1958), an Indianapolis native who was doing noteworthy etchings and lithographs in New York; and Ernest Thorne Thompson (b. 1897) of New Rochelle, New York. Though not a native of the state, Thompson had been the first director of the art department at Notre Dame from 1922 to 1928. He was the author of *Technique and the Modern Woodcut*, and one of his etchings had been chosen as one of the Fifty Prints of the Year in 1928. Doel Reed (b. 1894) also joined. Reed was born in Fulton County and had been one of the early Brown County painters, but his prowess as an aquatint artist developed after he had left Indiana to head the art department of Oklahoma A & M (Oklahoma State University) in Stillwater in 1925. Reed had first been exposed to etching while at the Cincinnati Art Academy where he witnessed L. H. Meakin pull prints from Frank Duveneck's etching plates presumably in 1915. By 1933, Reed was considered the country's finest aquatint etcher, and one of his works was among the Fifty Prints of the Year. Indiana resident members included Dorothy L. Eisenbach (b. 1899) of Lafayette, who had studied lithography at the Pennsylvania Academy of the Fine Arts in 1931, and C. M. Sonen (b. 1874), a woodcut specialist born in Germany who had worked in Indianapolis for many years as a commercial wood-engraver at a time when that medium was used extensively for magazine and newspaper illustration. Edmund Schildknecht and Walter McBride, mentioned above as Arsenal instructors, were also charter members, as was Charles G. Yeager (1910-1970), one of McBride's instructors at the Fort Wayne Art School. Yeager would later chair the art department at Shortridge High School in Indianapolis from 1938 to 1965.

Following the exhibition at Lieber's the society decided to circulate a smaller show to various colleges and galleries around the state. The first year the prints traveled to Franklin College, Fort Wayne, Logansport, Anderson, and Ball State in Muncie. The traveling show became an annual follow-up to the Members' Exhibit, and in 1935,

Purdue University, Richmond, and Marion were added to the itinerary.

Up to the beginning of World War II, through seven annual exhibitions at Lieber's and one at Herron, the membership of the society remained fairly constant. A few members became inactive and others took their places. Charles Surendorf (b. 1906) of Logansport began exhibiting with the society in its second year and continued to send block prints annually even after moving to Columbia, California, in 1937.

George Jo Mess became a member in 1936, showing four of his early aquatints. After they moved to Chicago in 1937 George and Evelynne continued to send prints to the annual exhibitions, including Evelynne's first lithographs in 1938, the products of her study under Francis Chapin at the Art Institute of Chicago. When they returned to Indianapolis in July, 1940, Evelynne resumed her duties as secretary of the society, replacing Constance Forsyth, who accepted a position teaching etching and lithography at the University of Texas at Austin that fall. William Schaldach (b. 1896), an Evansville native residing in West Hartford, Vermont, and a specialist in paintings of sporting interest, became a member and began contributing etchings and drypoints in 1937. Ella Fillmore Lillie (b. 1887), a fine lithographer, joined in 1938. She was born in Minneapolis, had studied at the Art Institute of Chicago and the New York School of Fine Arts, and was living in Danby, Vermont, when she joined the society. She qualified for membership by having spent several years in Indianapolis following World War I, when her husband worked as an engineer for the Stutz motorcar company. Lillie was a constant contributor to the annual members' exhibits. Floyd Hopper (1909-1984) sent block prints in 1936 and 1937, while still a student at the Herron Art Institute. In 1938 he sent lithographs. These were among the first examples of lithography produced at Herron.

In 1935 Donald M. Mattison (1905-1975), the new dean of the Herron art school, produced a lithograph entitled *Negro Baptism* concurrently with his well-known painting of the same subject. The lithograph was exhibited at the Art Institute of

Chicago's Annual International Exhibition of Lithography and Wood-Engraving that winter. In October, 1937, Mattison announced the purchase of a litho stone and press for Herron and formed a group of advanced students to study lithography as an extracurricular activity.[11] Faculty members participated as well. Mattison pulled a few more prints over the next few years as did fellow instructors Henrik Martin Mayer (1908-1972), David K. Rubins (b. 1902), and Edmund Brucker (b. 1912). The students working in lithography the first year included Floyd Hopper, Harry A. Davis (b. 1914), Edwin Fulwider (1913-1972), and Paul Wehr (1914-1973). For the most part their early lithographs were sketches for paintings in progress transferred to the litho stone for the purpose of multiplying a successful image. Examples of the lithographs were included in the annual student show at Herron in July, 1938.

In May, 1939, Mattison invited Max Kahn and Francis Chapin of the Art Institute of Chicago to come to Indianapolis for a four-week practical course in drawing on lithographic stone and printing open to third-, fourth-, and fifth-year students. Harrison "Misch" Kohn (b. 1916) was among the participants in the seminar. Kohn was so intrigued by the possibilities of printmaking that he left with Chapin for Chicago[12] and was soon established as one of the nation's most promising young printmakers.

The course was offered again in the spring of 1940 and taught by Kahn. Twelve examples of the students' work were seen at the student exhibit following the end of the seminar in June.

The quality of work produced by the Herron students was soon acknowledged. Edwin Fulwider had his own lithography studio in Brown County in 1939 before being hired to teach drawing and printmaking at Miami University in Ohio in 1942. Paul Wehr taught commercial art at Herron and had the "outstanding print" at the Hoosier Salon in 1941—a lithograph entitled *The Station*. Floyd Hopper's *Blue Monday* won first prize in the National Lithography Exhibition in Oklahoma City in 1940.

On November 12, 1941, Mattison announced

that a lithography course would be offered at the Herron Evening School, beginning with a lithography demonstration by Floyd Hopper.[13] Several students participated in this informal class, receiving technical assistance from Hopper and second-year student Garo Antreasian (b. 1922). Antreasian had been introduced to lithography while a high school student at Arsenal and carried his interest to Herron. In 1942 his lithograph *Aftermath* won the local award in the National Red Cross contest. Antreasian served in the Coast Guard during World War II and returned to Herron in 1946. His interest in color lithography was initiated by Maxil Ballinger (b. 1914), who had recently been hired as Indiana University's first graphics instructor. Antreasian joined the staff at Herron in 1948 to teach painting, design, and printmaking—becoming the first full-time instructor of printmaking. His appointment coincided with his receiving the Mary B. Milliken Award for Excellence, which financed two summers of advanced study in New York under such major printers as George Miller, Stanley William Hayter and his Atelier 17, and Will Barnet at the Art Students League.

The Indiana Society of Printmakers revived their annual exhibition schedule in November, 1944, after a two-year hiatus because of the war. It was their first Tri-State exhibition, including 171 prints from Indiana, Illinois, and Ohio. The exhibition was arranged by George Jo Mess and hung in Block's department store auditorium in downtown Indianapolis. A similar exhibition was mounted the following year and marked the first appearance of lithography by Herron faculty members Edmund Brucker and Donald Mattison. Both were invited to join the society as were David K. Rubins and Henrik Mayer, but only Brucker appears to have done so. In 1946 Garo Antreasian and Maxil Ballinger exhibited for the first time with the society, as did Terre Haute's Ray French (b. 1919), who was then studying under master intaglio printmaker Mauricio Lasansky at the University of Iowa. Another Lasansky student, Ernest B. Freed, born in Rockville in 1908, began exhibiting with the Society in 1950. Indianapolis native John Bernhardt (1921-1963) was a third young artist working

in a decidedly abstract manner who would rise to national prominence after the first exposure of his woodcuts with the society in 1950, following his graduation from Herron and his move to New York.

It was quite apparent that the Indiana Society of Printmakers, like printmaking in America in general, was moving in a new and experimental direction in the late forties. Garo Antreasian succeeded George Jo Mess as president in 1951, and the new prospectus written by the society signaled the changing times. "In the recent post war period," it noted, "a general and natural transition has occurred in our organization. Newer and younger names have been added to the membership list, bringing to the exhibitions vital and necessary impetus." The appeal to new members was clearly seen in the exhibition in 1952.

For the first time since 1937, the exhibition, in 1952, was held at the Herron Art Museum. It also marked the First Biennial Exhibition of 50 Indiana Prints which replaced the annual members' exhibit. Though many of the longtime members—Evelynne and George Jo Mess, Polley, Eisenbach, Griffith, Lillie, Schaldach, Reed, Surendorf, and Leich—were represented, the exhibition was dominated by the young lions. Antreasian, Ray French, Ernest Freed, and Misch Kohn took the top prizes. Indiana University Associate Professor George Rickey (b. 1907), the noted kinetic sculptor, exhibited one of the etchings he had recently completed while working under Lasansky. Arthur Deshaies (b. 1920), newly appointed graphics instructor at Indiana University, participated for the first time as did I. U. student James McGarrell of Indianapolis (b. 1930). Several of Antreasian's lithography students also debuted at this exhibition, including William Crutchfield (b. 1932). The early and continuing successes of these young printmakers established Indiana University and the John Herron Art Institute as leading centers for the study of fine printmaking[14]—a remarkable change from the situation Evelynne Bernloehr had encountered twenty years earlier.

The Indiana Society of Printmakers ceased to exist after the Second Biennial in 1954, though the biennials continued at Herron through the 1960s. In the course of its history the Society, Evelynne Mess's brain-child, had more than fulfilled its expectations. Its twenty years of success had been due largely to the devotion and diligence of Evelynne and George Jo Mess. As intended from the beginning, the Indiana Society of Printmakers had brought the first exposure of fine and original prints to many of the state's residents. Perhaps not as clearly foreseen in 1934, the Society had provided the first forum for a new generation of graphic artists who would figure among the most distinguished printmakers, teachers, and technicians in postwar America.

Evelynne's and George's etchings and aquatints accepted for national exhibitions, awarded national honors, and entered in public collections are sufficient to secure their places in Indiana art. But, their most enduring contribution is perhaps less easy to quantify. It is significantly to their credit that the prevailing prejudice against printmaking as a minor art was broken and the psychological barrier against printmaking as an occupation was breached. They achieved this by their own example and by their organization and stewardship of the Indiana Society of Printmakers. For the two decades after its founding in 1934 the Indiana Society of Printmakers was the first, the major, and the only consistent outlet for the best printmakers in the state.

Notes

1. W. Forsyth, *Art in Indiana* (Indianapolis: H. Lieber Co., 1916), pp. 12-13. Forsyth unfortunately does not specify what motivated the members of the Bohe Club to take up etching. It cannot be coincidental that their first efforts coincide precisely with the first stirrings of etching as an original art throughout the country around 1880. P. G. Hamerton's pioneering treatise *Etching and Etchers* appeared in 1868, followed by the first English translation of Maxime Lalanne's 1866 *A Treatise on Etching* in 1880. The New York Etching Club was founded in 1877, followed by similar associations in Cincinnati, Philadelphia, Boston, and Brooklyn within five years. The first comprehensive study of America's new fascination with etching was written by S. R. Koehler and was published as a series of articles in *The American Art Review* in 1880. By at least 1885 "fine etch-

ings and engravings" were available in Indianapolis at the H. Lieber Art Emporium (founded 1854), according to an advertisement on the back cover of their catalogue of the *Art Exhibit of ye Hoosier Colony in Munchen*, illustrated, incidentally, by Bohe Club members T. E. Hibben, F. A. Hetherington, W. Forsyth, and Charles A. Nicolai.

2. There is no evidence to disprove Forsyth's statement, though prints of Indiana, published elsewhere, had appeared before 1880. These were primarily views of the Indiana wilderness printed by traveling artists in the middle years of the nineteenth century. Basil Hall (Scottish, 1788-1844) included two views along the Ohio River in Indiana in his *Forty Etchings from Sketches made with the Camera Lucida in North America in 1827 and 1828*; Carl Bodmer (Swiss, 1809-1893) engraved several of the drawings he had made in New Harmony in 1834; William Momberger (German, b. 1820) included three hand-colored engravings of Indiana scenes in his 1869 *National Gallery of American Landscape*. See Wilbur Peat, *Pioneer Painters of Indiana* (Indianapolis: Art Association of Indianapolis, 1954), pp. 11-13. To these can be added Alexander H. Ritchie's (1822-1895) engraved interpretation of Miss J. Hamilton's painting of *The Ohio River, Hanover College* printed around 1870.

3. Indianapolis *Star*, August 21, 1927.

4. *New Era Magazine*, March 9, 1912, p. 11.

5. Forsyth appears to have exhibited his etchings only once during his lifetime. In late November, 1913, he showed etchings at the gallery of the Woman's Department Club in Indianapolis along with some of his recent paintings. After his death in 1934 several of his etchings were added to the memorial exhibition of his paintings at the Herron Art Institute. J. Ottis Adams's memorial exhibition at Herron in October, 1927, marked the only public exposure of his etchings, six of his "Munich period" prints being included.

6. Remarks made on October 17, 1933, on the occasion of an exhibition of the Brown County artists at the Hoosier Gallery (Indianapolis Museum of Art, Archives).

7. Gustave Baumann to Calla Hay in "Gustave Baumann," *El Palacio*, LXXVII, No. 1, 1972, p. 27. Baumann added that "Life [in Brown County] was simple. I could stay for two months for $100."

8. Indianapolis *News*, October 28, 1922.

9. Indianapolis *Star*, November 13, 1932.

10. There were notable exceptions. Forsyth showed his etchings at the Woman's Department Club in 1913 as noted above (note 5); Gustave Baumann's first Indiana one-man show was held there in February, 1913, as was the first exhibition of Frederick Polley's Indianapolis etchings in November of that same year. In January, 1922, fifteen of Polley's etchings joined sixteen of his paintings in an exhibition at the club.

11. Indianapolis *Star*, October 22, 1937; *Art Association of Indianapolis Annual Reports for the Years 1936 and 1937* (Indianapolis: John Herron Art Institute, 1938), p. 19.

12. Carl Zigroseer, *Misch Kohn* (New York: The American Federation of Arts, 1961), p. 5.

13. Indianapolis *Times*, November 12, 1941.

14. Among other prestigious awards, these young Indiana printmakers took eleven of the first one hundred and seventy-seven purchase prizes at the most influential National Print Annual exhibitions at the Brooklyn Museum from the first in 1947 through the twelfth in 1960: Maxil Ballinger (1947), Ernest Freed (1947), Misch Kohn (1950 and 1951), Arthur Deshaies (1950 and 1956), John Bernhardt (1954), James McGarrell (1955), and Garo Antreasian (1960).

Evelynne Bernloehr gained her first practical exposure to the art of etching in a 1924 class conducted by Frederick Polley at the John Herron Art Institute when she, along with other class members, contributed lines to a plate for this print.

Works in Permanent Collections

George Jo Mess

Philadelphia Museum of Art
(aquatints)
All Is Quiet, 1950
Crucifixion, 1958
Driftwood, 1946
Ever So Humble, 1937
Four O'Clock, 1943
The Goat Farm, 1944
The Handy Pump, 1954
In Full Moon, 1957
Living Better Without, 1945
Main Street, 1947
Minnows, 1953
New Dawn, 1943
Picnic, 1953
Reelsfoot Bridge, 1939
Scarecrow, 1952
Snowbound, 1936
Weather Vane, 1953

Library of Congress
(aquatints)
Backyard Romance, 1936
Living Better Without, 1945
Lullaby of the Leaves, 1945
Old Fairland Mill, 1940
Prairie Pump, 1940
Summer Solitude, 1941
Time for Rest, 1939
Twins, 1953

James E. Roberts School for Crippled Children, Indianapolis
(aquatints)
Abode of the Boatmaker, 1935
The Barren Plum Tree, 1935
Edge of the Forest, 1935
Prevailing Winds, 1935
Snowbound, 1936
Southern Oak, 1936

Indianapolis Museum of Art
(aquatints)
Abode of the Boatmaker, 1935
Aurora, 1935
Backyard Romance, 1936
The Barren Plum Tree, 1935
Bayfield, 1939
Christmas Eve, 1936
City of Rooftops, 1938
Coastline, 1939
Coffee Time, 1951
Covered Bridge, 1949
Dawn, 1941
Driftwood, 1946
Ed Luckey's Farm, 1937
Edge of the Forest, 1935
Ever So Humble, 1937
The Forge, 1941
Four O'Clock, 1943
Garden of Eve, 1937
Glorious Day, 1941
The Goat Farm, 1944
The Handy Pump, 1943
Highway Number Seven, 1951
If Winter Comes, 1939
Living Better Without, 1945
Magnitude, 1937
Main Street, 1947

Metamora, 1935
Moonlight Sailing, 1941
Nashville Courthouse, 1936
Neighbors, 1940
Nestled in the Hills, 1935
Old Fairland Mill, 1940
Palmolive Building, 1938-1940
Pose, 1937
Prevailing Winds, 1935
Sand Dune Cabins, 1940
Sawmill, 1949
Snowbound, 1936
Southern Oak, 1936
Time for Rest, 1939
Where Bridges Meet, 1941
Winter Moonlight, 1939
Wishing Gate, 1937
Work-shed, 1939

(paintings)
Farm House Interior, 1942, oil
On Tiffany's Estate, 1931, oil
Sail Boat Harbor, 1957, watercolor
Will-o-the Wisp, 1955, oil & devolac

Cleveland Museum of Art
Wishing Gate, 1937, aquatint

Metropolitan Museum of Art
Highway Number Seven, 1951, aquatint

Princeton University Museum
Wishing Gate, 1937, aquatint

Richmond Art Association, Richmond, Indiana
The Handy Pump, 1954, aquatint

South Bend Art Association
Metamora, 1930, oil

Indiana University Medical Center
Coffee Time, 1951, aquatint
Goat Farm, 1944, aquatint
Living Better Without, 1945, aquatint

Indiana State Museum
Lake of Abandoned Strip Mine, 1947, oil

Broad Ripple High School
Christmas Eve, 1936, aquatint
Ever So Humble, 1937, aquatint
Main Street at Wadham, 1947, watercolor

Evelynne Mess Daily

Philadelphia Museum of Art
Adirondack Trail, 1945, aquatint
Branching Willow, 1934, aquatint

Library of Congress
Adirondack Trail, 1945, aquatint

Fort Wayne Art Museum
Branching Willow, 1934, aquatint

Richmond Art Association, Richmond, Indiana
Branching Willow, 1934, aquatint

DePauw University
Cornflowers and Dill, 1963, oil
Leaves, 1964, oil

Indiana State Museum
Indiana Limestone Quarry, 1974, lithograph

Indianapolis Museum of Art
Adirondack Trail, 1945, aquatint
Back Yard in Episy, 1929, etching
Barnyard Controversy, 1949, aquatint-etching
Boat House, 1938, lithograph
Boats on Lake Lugano, 1930, aquatint
Branching Willow, 1934, aquatint
Brookville Church, 1934, aquatint
Country Kitchen, 1973, lithograph
Deserted Log Cabins, 1969, etching
Design from a Frosted Window, 1934, aquatint
Feasting, 1948, aquatint-etching
Holiday in the Country, 1948, aquatint
Hotel de Ville, 1929, drypoint
In the Bay, 1935, etching
Lakeside Barn, 1980, oil
Limestone Quarry, 1974, lithograph
Mother and Babes, 1947, lithograph
Old Montmarte, 1929, etching
Porte de Samois, 1929, etching
Rainy Day in Fontainebleau, 1929, drypoint
Street Musicians, 1929, etching
Toadstools, 1940, etching
Towers of the Alps, 1930, etching
Water Fantasy, Nymph, 1931, aquatint
Winding Road, 1935, aquatint-etching
Winter Night, 1936, aquatint

Indiana State Library
Adirondack Trial, 1945, aquatint

Works of Evelynne Mess Daily

Paintings

(All works are oil paintings
unless otherwise designated.)

1925, *Summer Landscape*
Nude
1927, *Toadstools*
1928, *The Narrows, Cumberland*
1929, *Along the Old Canal*
Mountain Barnyard
The Old Barn
Toll Bridge at Moret
Village of Montigny
Wash Day at Moret
1930, *Canal Houses*
1931, *Still Life with Daisies*
1933, *Towers in Moret*
1935, *The Bernloehr Brothers*
1941, *Still Life*
1942, *Morels*
1943, *Arrangement*
Still Life (Mt. Laurel & jug)
1944, *Little Mary and Her Doll*
Mountain View, watercolor
Rebecca
The Violinist
1945, *Butterfly Plants & Daisies*
Little Faces
Mountain Bouquet
Native (an Adirondack tree
farmer)
The Native (a Brown County
native)
Red Barn & Silo
White Mountain Flowers

1946, *Brown County Farmer*
Country Church (Brookville)
Early Bloom, watercolor
Mushrooms
Portrait of Old Man
Rocks, watercolor
1947, *Asters & Ageratum*
Babe in the Woods
Flower Arrangement
Flowers with Treasure Chest
Hillside Farm, watercolor
Northern Wood, watercolor
S Curves
1948, *Carnivorous Plant,*
watercolor
Chanterella with Gypsy Moth
Fountain of Youth
Life on Our Farm
Lilies for Easter
Morels and Tinderwood
Mushrooms, watercolor
Old Fashioned Bouquet
The Preyer
1949, *Chipmunks at Play*
Committee Women
Dandelions
On Parade
1950, *Farmer Friend*
Walking in the Rain
1951, *Boulder Valley*, watercolor
Bromelia, watercolor
December in the Village
Evening Bonfire
Lake Shore, watercolor
Land of Nod
Mushroom Hollow
Nosegay

1952, *Cucurbita*
December
Family Circle
Lumber Mill, watercolor
Magic Touch of Winter
Make Believe
Upland Glen, watercolor
1953, *Arrangement with Real*
Butterfly, collage
1954, *Glorious Day*
Herbs in My Garden,
formerly *Herbs Gone to*
Seed
The Islands, watercolor
1955, *Calendula Leaves*, watercolor
Lazy River, watercolor
Mardi Gras
Snow Covered Tree,
watercolor
Summer Landscape
Under the Mulberry Tree,
watercolor
Water Fantasy
Water Lilies
Winter Haven, formerly
Feathered Snow
1956, *Blue Jay*
Easter Lily
In My Studio
Indian Pipes, acrylic
watercolor
Still Life
1957, *Aquarium*
Fascinating Fungi, watercolor
Field Flowers
Foot Bridge, watercolor
Garden Still Life, watercolor

Hidden Mushrooms
Illusive Ones
Spider Plant
Still Life with Jug and Bottles
Woodland Mushrooms
1958, *Abstract*, watercolor airbrush
Chef's Delight
Flower Fragments, watercolor
Oxbow Acres Bridge
Pink Poppies
Undisturbed
1959, *Carnivorous Plant*,
    watercolor
Copper Pitcher
Fall Creek Romance
Seed Pods
Sunset
1960, *Covered Bridge (Autumn*
    Glory)
Eve's Farm Kitchen,
    watercolor
Haven for Praying Mantis
Hillside at Oxbow Acres
Money Plant and Oranges
Monument on the Circle
Poke Berries
Poke Berries II, watercolor
Still Life
1961, *Blossom Time*
Bridge to Shangrila
Butterfly's Treat
Christmas Tree Farm
    (Evergreen Hills)
Flowers and Fruit
Her Summer Home
Lobster
Snow in the Hills
Wild Blossoms, watercolor
1962, *Arrangement with Treasure*
    Chest
Covered Bridge
Mixed Bouquet
1963, *Autumn in Brown County*
Cornflowers & Dill
Italian Bowl and Bottle
Turbulence, oil & devolac

1964, *Brown County Squashes*
Leaves
Silvia Selkirk
Stairway to the Stars
Summer Landscape
Untitled (Abstract), airbrush
    watercolor
Waiting to Go
1965, *Bowl of Mushrooms with Jug*,
    watercolor
Early Blooms, watercolor
Fall Landscape
Florida Grass & Dill
Florida Grass with Money
    Plant
Hideaway
Spring Blossoms, watercolor
Summertime
1966, *Indian Chief*
A Lovely Day for Ducks or
    Rain Storm
Woodland Treasures, collage
1967, *Dinner Bell*
Mending Fishnets
Sand Dunes
Tropicana, watercolor
1968, *Aquatic Composition*, mixed
    medium
Autumn Woodland
Berries and Blossoms,
    watercolor
Collage
Late Summer Landscape
Nature Collage
Old Apartments
Queen Anne's Lace, collage
Rooftops, watercolor
The Yellow Maple
1969, *Antique Kitchen Stove*
Glorious Day for Fishing
Haven for Wildlife
Kitchen Still Life
Little Carmen
Still Life (bowl of grapes &
    blue bottles)
Summer in Hills
1970, *Bottle Collection*
Butterfly Plant and Seed Pods
Cloudburst

Edge of the Forest,
    watercolor
Fisherman's Cove, watercolor
Fishing Lure, watercolor
    airbrush
Silent Cloak of Winter
Solitude
Under a Blanket of Snow, oil
Variation, formerly *Abstract*
    Design, watercolor
    airbrush
Village in December
Wild Flowers (Lady Slippers)
1971, *Abstract*, watercolor airbrush
Arrangement in Red, White,
    & Blue, collage
Butterfly Plant
December Snow
February Snow, watercolor
Grandmother's Organ
Snow Storm
1972, *Duck Season*, watercolor
Her Antique Corner, pastel
Lilies with Passion Flower
Lily Pond
Lone Pine
On the Back Porch
Orientals
Road to Romance
Winter Wonderland
1973, *Barnyard Corral*, watercolor
Beechwoods
Fading Barns, watercolor
The Flight, watercolor
Mushrooms
Singing Pines
Stormy Weather, formerly
    The Blizzard
1975, *Glorious Day*
Indiana Limestone Quarry
Neighbors' Barns
Tiger, watercolor
Yellow Covered Bridge,
    pastel
1976, *Blossom Time*
January Snow
Wild Parsnips & Cornflowers
1977, *Aurora*
Leaves in the Landscape,
    collage

1978, *Blizzard of '78*
    Garden for Songbirds
    Old Town (France),
        watercolor
    Plant Life
    Variations
1979, *Cypress Lodge*
1980, *Down on the Farm*
    Lakeside Barn
    Nature Collage, formerly
        Illusive Ones, collage
    Oxbow Acres Barn
1981, *An Autumn Day*
    Butterfly on a Log
    End of Day
    Hang Gliding
    Metropolitan Opera House
    Old Homestead, watercolor
    Pholioto (Mushroom)
1982, *Antique Kitchen,* watercolor
    Bridge Road
    Caladium Plant, watercolor
    Dandelion Plant, watercolor
    Early Autumn
    Eucalyptus, formerly *Forms*
        in Space, oil & devolac
    Home in the Hills
    January
    Miles of Landscape
    Winter Wonderland
1983, *Bottle Collection*
    Bridge at Madison
    Canal Houses, watercolor
    Decorative Composition,
        watercolor airbrush
    Gold Fish, watercolor
    Rainy Day
    Snow Covered Tree
    Tiger, watercolor
    Triangle
1984, *Along the Canal*
    Blossoms and Butterflies
    City Streets
    Ducks' Playground,
        watercolor
    Sand Dunes
    Silent Woods, watercolor
    Tiger Lily, watercolor

Undated Paintings
    Brown County Valley
    Jenny Wren's Home
    Landscape with Pheasants,
        mural
    Pansies
    Sunset Hill

Prints

A   aquatint
AE   aquatint-etching
B   blockprint
E   etching
D   drypoint
W   woodcut
L   lithograph
S   serigraph

1928, *Central Avenue Studio,* E
1929, *Along the Arno, Florence,*
       Italy, E
    Back Yard in Episy
       (France), E
    Courtyard in Moret, E
    Hotel de Ville, D
    Old Montmarte, E
    Porte de Samois, E
    Rainy Day in Fontaine-
       bleau, D
    Street Musicians, E
    Trees of Fontainebleau, E
1930, *Amelitia,* D
    Boats on Lake Lugano, E
    [Book Plates] (for Mary Q.
       Burnet, Woman's
       Department Club, Marian
       and Boris Medich, Arthur
       Baxter Gipe, John Daily,
       and Evelynne Mess), E
    Grossmunster Cathedral, E
    Towers of the Alps, E
1931, *Water Fantasy, Nymph,* A
1932, *Country Church,* B
    In Brown County, W
    Queen Anne's Lace, E
    Toilers of France, E

1934, *Along White River,* E
    Boat House, E
    Branching Willow, A
    Brookville Church, A
    Brown County, Indiana, W
    Church in China, Indiana, E
    Country Home in Edge-
       wood, B
    Covered Bridge, E
    Design from a Frosted
       Window, A
    Lakeside, E
    Landscape Composition,
       monotype
    Tangled Branches, D
    Under a Blanket of Snow, A
    Water Fantasy, Sea Horse, A
1935, *In the Bay,* E
    Nature's Lacework, AE
    Rooster, B
    Rugged Individual, A
    Self Portrait, E
    Wild Flowers, B
    Winding Road, AE
1936, *Alabama Row,* B
    Barnyard Beauty, W
    Lilies of the Field, W
    Sleepy Hollow, E
    Winter Night, A (*Rainy Day*
       in Fontainebleau with
       aquatint added)
1937, *Wash Day in Moret,* B
1938, *Boat House,* L
    My Pets, L
    Night Club Lights, L
    River Camp, L
1939, *Along the Arno, Florence,* L
    Street Vendors, B
    Wren's Gourd House, A
       (min)
1940, *Potters,* L
    Toadstools, E
1942, *Christmas Tree,* L
1944, *Adirondack Valley Farm,* L
    Bird's Nest, L
    By the Old Apple Trees, L
    Feeding Time, L
    Lake Placid, E

Landscape in Miniature, A
Old Apple Trees, L
Valley Farm, L
1945, *Adirondack Trail*, A
Mountain Valley Farm, L
1946, *Country Church*, E
In the Mountains, E
Terraced Farm, L
1947, *Abandoned Bridge*, AE,
    color
Mother and Babes (I), L
Summer Day, E (min)
1948, *Feasting*, AE
Holiday in the Country, A
One Summer Day, A
1949, *Barnyard Controversy*, AE
1950, *Birches*, E (min)
Lone Pine, E (min)
Snow-Clad Tree, A
1959, *Aquarium*, W
1950s, *Beautiful but Dangerous*, S
Garden of Flowers, S
Mushrooms, S
1969, *Apple Trees*, E
Deserted Log Cabins, E
1970, *Grossmunster Cathedral*, L
Happy Frogs, L
Parasol Mushrooms, L
1971, *Snails on Psaliota*, L
1972, *Passion Flower*, L
Tortoise, L
Who-o-s Who (Great Horned
    Owl), L
1973, *Book of Daniel*, collograph
Country Kitchen, L
Mother and Babes (II), L
Pot-Belly Stove, L
1974, *Indiana Limestone Quarry*, L
1975, *Coral Reef*, A
1977, *Passion Vine*, E
Praying Mantis, E
1970s, *Abstracts*, L
1982, *Dr. Mayo's House*, A
Sans End, E

Works of George Jo Mess

Paintings

(All works are oil paintings
unless otherwise designated.)

1917, *Good Fishing*
1918, *After the Snow*
1925, *First Snow*
    Snow Covered City
1926, *Early Days in Indianapolis*
    Indianapolis in the 20s
    October Sunshine
1927, *Broad Ripple Bridge*
    Broad Ripple Dam
    Summer Patterns
1928, *Autumn*, pastel
    Brown County
    Moonlight
1929, *Across the Canal of Episy*
    Along a Canal in France
    Among the Hills
    Clouds of France
    Decoration at Fontainebleau
      (Decoration)
    Fontainebleau Woods
    Forest of Fontainebleau
    In the Hills of Villecerf
    In the Valley
    Mill at Montigny
    Mill of Moret
    Montigny from the Hill Top
    Reflection of Episy
    Southern France
    Winter in Indianapolis
1930, *Brown County Farm Yard*
    Canal Moret
    Chateau Country
    Church of Montigny

Decorative Trees (Long
    Island, N.Y.)
Gardener's House,
    watercolor
Metamora
Red Iron Bridge
Village of Moret
Village of Villecerf
1931, *Brookside Bridge*
    Buildings
    Cold Springs Harbor
    In the Garden of Paradise
    Indianapolis in Snow
    Industrial Indianapolis
    Long Island Landscape
    Long Island Trees
    On Tiffany's Estate
    Oyster Bay, Long Island
    Tiffany's Front Yard
    Valley of Tile Roofs
1932, *Brown County Farm*
    A Century of Progress (*Bridge
      at Madison*) (*To the Hills
      of Kentucky*)
    Church in China
    Country Church (Long
      Island, N.Y.)
    Flat Rock at Night
    Fontainebleau Hotel,
      watercolor
    A Glorious Day
    The Last Snow
    The Mystery Shack
    New Augusta Church
    *Normandy Farm, New
      Augusta, Indiana*
    Reelsfoot Lake, watercolor

The Road Turns
Self-Portrait
Street Fair
1933, *Gas Plant*
    Geraniums
    Old Iron Sides
    Swimming Party
    Tapestry Season, watercolor
    To the Beach
    Twins
1934, *Across the Ohio*
    Along White River
    Hill Homestead
    The Lanier Home
    Nashville
    Notre Dame Cathedral
    Pink Estate
    Red Silo
    Sunday
1935, *Along the Ohio River*
    Aurora
    Kentucky Hills and Apples
    Romantic Aurora
    The Stag
1937, *Backyard Romance*
    Boy Fishing (small sketch)
    Ed Luckey's Farm
    Passing of the Monarch
    Storm in Aurora
    The Village Road
1938, *Around the Hill Top*
    Homeward Bound
    Indiana Lime Stone Quarries
    Nashville (min)
    Palmolive Building
    Sand and Concrete
    Walton Place

1939, *Artist's Holiday*
Dunes
Lake View #1
Lake View #2
Namakogan Lake
Neighbors at the Dunes
Seascape
The Work Shop, opaque
watercolor
1930s, "Fairyland" (illustration for
children's book)
1940, *Bridge over Clay Lick (Clay
Lick Bridge)*
Eve on the Beach, watercolor
1941, *Dawn*
Mac's Cabin, Brown County
Phantasy II
Stairway to the Sky
1942, *Adirondack Solitude*
Brown County Church
Farm House Interior
Long Island Bay
Neighbor's Farm
Nestled in the Hills
Pioneer Life
Sunset Hill
Time for Rest
Yellow Wood Lake
1943, *Ever So Humble*
Joe's Backyard
Nashville Courthouse
Red Barn
Summer Kitchen
Summer Romance
1944, *Adirondack Mountain*
Adirondack Rocks & Pines
Adirondacks
Adirondacks near Lake Placid
After the Shower
Around the Mountains
Booth Fisheries
Clay Lick Road
Clay Lick Valley
Contented Valley
Floating Clouds
Heavy Snow
Hill Side
House of Mr. Charles Coats
Indiana Quarry
Lakes in Summer

Little Falls
Long Shadows
Mountain Romance
Mountaineer Home
Mystic Morning
Noontime in the Mountains
Poetic Pines
Solitude in the Mountains
Summer in the Adirondacks
Sunset in the Adirondacks
Sunshine and Shadows
When Day is Done
White Pine Ridge
1945, *Bridge over Brook*
Brook
Camp Fire Joy
Cherry Tree
Down by the Creek
Fall Morning
Gold & Blue
Hill Country
Hill Top Pond
Home Sweet Home
Lake Placid
Morning Mist
Mountain Farm
Old Homestead
Outing
Outlook
Pond
Road to Lake
Road's End
Salt Creek
Saw Mill
Shore Line
Small Brook
Springtime
Still Life
Trout Brook
Valley
Very Old Barn
Wayman Adams Mill Village
1946, *Abode of the Boatmaker*
Adirondack View
Beyond
Early Autumn
The Long Ford
Orchard View
The Promise
White Pine

Yellow Barn
1947, *Allisonville*
Bill's Farm
Blue Roofs
Bouquet River Romance
Brown County Hill Top
Brown County Valley
Deserted Strip Mine
Early Fall
*Fall Creek Mill (Schofield
Mill) (The Old Mill)*
Gravel Pit
Handy Pump
Hill Roads
Hill Top Pond
In the Hills
Indiana Lake Farm
Just a Fishin
Lake in the Hill
*Lake of Abandoned Strip
Mine*
Lake Region
Late Fall
The Lonely Road
Lost Trail
Love
Main Street at Wadham,
watercolor
Meditation
Our Country Studio
River's Crest
Scrapple Hollow
*Snow in the Mountains (Snow
in the Adirondacks)*
Summer Time
Winter in the Hills
1946-1948, *In the Adirondacks*
Wisconsin Lake
1948, *Cove*
Embers
Foothills
The Heart of a Woman
Hideout
Lakeside
Mountain Serenity
Mountain View
Passing Storm
Pond on the Hill
Population 514
Tapestry, watercolor

Village of Wadham,
watercolor
The Yellow House
1949, *Clay Lick Slabs*
Lake in the Hills
A Passing Cloud
Picnic
Reelsfoot, watercolor
1950, *Atomic Age*
Clearing Skies
Golden Hill
Green Valley
Highway Number Seven
Little Red Iron Bridge
Paradise Valley
Reelsfoot Bayou
Snow in My Valley
Yellow Covered Bridge
1951, *Abstract,* watercolor
Autumn Bouquet
Dead End Street
Fall Cleanup
Feathered Quartette,
watercolor
Hitch Hikers
Into the Orchard
Leaves, watercolor
Open Road
Oriental Landscape,
watercolor
Pennsylvania Farm
Picnic in the Farm Yard
Poetic Lane
River Town
Running Wild
Time to Play
Vista
1952, *Coast Home*
Full Moon
Our Road
Sail Boat Regatta
Scarecrow
Signs of Good Time
Stormy Weather
1953, *Autumn Glory*
Fall Bouquet
Farm Backyard
Haunted Lot
Indiana Pageantry
Late Evening

Little Farm
October in Indiana
Retreat
Snow
Summer Home
Sympathetic Scarecrow
Variations
You Must Open the Door
1954, *Bit of Dill*
Branching Out
Brown County Landscape,
watercolor
High Water in Belleville
Mixed Bouquet
Terraced Farm
1955, *Bantams*
Ignus Fatuus (Will-o-the-
Wisp), oil & devolac
In the Garden, oil & devolac
Lake near Bean Blossom
Land o' Lakes, watercolor
Little Water Falls
Mardi Gras
New World, watercolor
Still Life in a Barn
Winter Patterns
Wishing Well by Walk,
watercolor
1956, *Back Roads,* watercolor
The Dancer, oil, lacquer
Dry Dock, Geist Lake
The Grape Vine, watercolor
Landscape (Carothers farm)
Radiant Autumn
Rugged Hills, watercolor
Wild Flowers, watercolor
1957, *Boat Harbor*
Indianapolis Boat Harbor
Limestone Quarry
Ping's Pond, watercolor
Quartette, watercolor
Sail Boat Harbor, watercolor
Shack in Brown County,
watercolor
To Sail Beyond
Wet Evening
1958, *Beach Picnic*
Blue Vase
Early Spring Patterns
Harbor Fantasia

Humble Living
Monument Circle (Monument
on the Circle)
The Old Swimmin Hole
Oyster House
Treasure Island, oil &
devolac
Winter Sun
1959, *After the Shower,* watercolor
Brown County Courthouse
Brown County Farmhouse,
watercolor
Cozy
Crooked Creek Valley
Early Thaw
Echo Hills
Fisherman's Lore, watercolor
Hibiscus
Italian Zucchini
Little Church
Midsummer Night's Dream,
oil & devolac
New Horizons
Orange Lily
Overlook
Rags to Riches
Side Yard
1960, *Brown County Cabin*
Brown County Stream
Early Budding
In the Bay
Lady Bird
Large Valley
Lonely Trail
Musical Echoes, oil & devolac
Ranch Home
Sound Waves over City Skies,
oil, lacquer
Spring in Brown County
Still Life, Queen Anne's Lace
Stone Head
Stone Head Valley
Sweet Peas in White Pitcher
Wine Berries, watercolor
1961, *Beside the Still Waters*
Christ Church
Faith
Forms of Leaf and Rock
Plant Life in Moonlight
Portrait of Two Birds

Rural Patterns
Sand Slopes
Way of Life
Undated Paintings
    Along the Ohio River
    At the Farm
    Autumn Landscape
    Autumn Romance,
      watercolor
    Avenue of Trees
    Flowers and Fruit
    Glorious Autumn
    The Island
    Landscape in January
    Landscape of Brown County
    Landscape with Horses
    Little Landscape
    The Lone Pine
    Melting Snow
    New Harmony
    The Old Barn
    Panorama
    Peach Blossoms
    Peach Orchard
    Pine Tree
    Pine Ridge
    Red Barn and Silo
    Rock Garden
    Romance
    To the Creek
    Water, Earth, and Heaven
    Winter in Brown County

Prints

A   aquatint
B   block print
E   etching

1935, *Abode of the Boatmaker*, A
    Aurora, A
    Barren Plum Tree, A
    Edge of the Forest, A
    Gardener's House, A
    Lightning, A (later re-etched
      as *Flashes in the Harbor*,
      1946)
    Metamora, A
    Nestled in the Hills, A
    The Open Road, A

Prevailing Winds, A
Summertime, A
A Trail, E
1936, *Backyard Romance*, A
    Christmas Eve, A
    Deep Shadows, mezzotint
    Landmark (Dead Sentinel), A
    Nashville Courthouse, A
    Snowbound, A
    Southern Oak, A
1937, *Agnus Dei*, A
    Breezes, A
    Dreaming, A
    Ed Luckey's Farm, A
    Enchanted Evening, A
    Enchanted Pool, A
    End of Trail, A
    Ever So Humble, A
    Garden of Eve, A
    The Hen, A
    In My Studio, A
    Lost Horizon, A
    Magnitude, A
    Moonlight & Shadows, A
    Music in the Air, A
    Pose, A
    Rural Delivery, A
    Sheltered Pool, A
    Southern Bayou, A
    Wishing Gate, A
    Within the Shadows, A
1938, *Barnyard*, A (min)
    Chicago, A
    City of Rooftops, A
    Flat Bayou, A
    Flower of the Dunes, A
    From a Rooftop, A
    The Goal, B
    The Hitching Post, A
    *Locket for a Very Young
      Girl*, A
    Medallion, A
    Resting, A
    Rites, A
    To Lucasta, A
    Tree, A (min)
    Twins, A (colts)
    Two Stars, A
    A Visitor from Delphi, A
      (min)

Watcher of the Skies, A
*You Who Regret the
    Leaves*, A
1938-1940, *Palmolive Building*, A
1939, *Bayfield*, A
    Coastline, A
    Fisheries, A
    Footbridge, A
    Hill Top, A
    If Winter Comes, A
    Love in a Chimney, A
    Reelsfoot Bridge, A
    Time for Rest, A
    Winter Moonlight, A
    Work-shed, A
1940, *All Parents Know*, A
    Christmas, A
    Driftwood, A (min)
    Faun, A (min)
    Ice House, A (min)
    Lake Superior, A
    Lullaby, A
    Neighbors, A
    Old Fairland Mill, A
    Outward Bound, A (min)
    Prairie Pump, A (min)
    Sand Dune Cabins, A
    Self-Portrait, A
    Singing Hill, A
    Sleigh Ride, A
    Snow Drifts, A (min)
    Tangled Branches, A
    Tracks, A (min)
    Winter, A
    Winter in the Hills, A
    Wishing Gate in Winter, A
1941, *Bellsville*, A
    Christmas, A (min)
    Dawn, A
    Eventide, A (min)
    The Farm, A
    The Forge, A
    Full Moon, A
    *Glorious Day (Summer-
      time)*, A
    Heavy Snow, A
    Moon Beams, A
    Moonlight Sailing, A
    Spring, A (min)
    Spring Morning, A (min)

Summer Solitude, A
Tropical Flower, A
Water Falls, A (min)
Where Bridges Meet, A
Winter Magic, A
1942, *Barns*, A
Strawberry Barrel, A (min)
Winter Night, A
1943, *Four O'Clock*, A
The Handy Pump, A
The House, A
A New Dawn, A
1944, *Adirondacks*, A
Goat Farm, A
1945, *Living Better Without*, A
Lullaby of the Leaves, A
1946, *Driftwood*, A
Flashes in the Harbor, A
Stanhope Hall, A
1947, *Family of Deer*, A
Family of Rabbits, A
Heavy Snow, B
Light Snow, B
Main Street, A
1949, *Covered Bridge*, A
Old Iron Bridge, A
Sawmill, A
1950, *All Is Quiet*, A
Barn, A (min)
Bean Blossom Bridge, A
Church at Night, A (min)
Haven of Rest, A
Winter Evening, A
Winter Twilight, A
1951, *Coffee Time*, A
Feathered Quartette, A
Highway No. Seven, A
Off the Main Highway, A
1952, *Bonnets*, A
Scarecrow, A
1953, *Gristmill*, A, color
Minnows, A
Picnic, A, color
Twins (twilight), A
Weather Vane, A
1954, *Brown County*, A
Brown County Estate, A
Covered Well, A, color
Handy Pump, A, color
Sorghum Mill, A, color

1955, *Dramatic Masks*, A
The Lighted Way, A
Moonbeam Rhythms, A
1956, *Early Spring*, A
Good Friday, A
1957, *Do Come Around*, A
In Full Moon, A
1958, *Crucifixion*, A
Spring, A
Twins Footbridge, A
1960, *Feathered Promenade*, A
Foot Bridge, A
Harvest, A
Winter on the Farm, A

Index

Happy Frogs, 92; *Haven for Wildlife*, 92; *Holiday in the Country*, 91-92; *In My Studio*, 75, 91; *In the Mountains*, 74; *Indiana Limestone Quarry*, 92, 93; *Kitchen Still Life*, 92; *Lake Shore*, 75; *Lakeside Barn*, 93; *Leaves*, 91; *Lilies of the Field*, 41; *Magic Touch of Winter*, 91; *Montmarte*, 28; *Mother and Babes*, 92; *The Narrows, Cumberland, Maryland*, 19; *Nature's Lacework*, 64; *Old Fashioned Bouquet*, 74; *Old Montmarte*, 28; *Old Town*, 93; *Parasol Mushrooms*, 92; *Passion Flower*, 92; *Porte de Samois*, 28; *Pot-Belly Stove*, 92; *Praying Mantis*, 92; *Rainy Day in Fontainebleau*, 28; *Sans End*, 92; *Seed Pods*, 92; *Summertime*, 92; *Toadstools*, 54, 92; *Towers of the Alps*, 28; *Trees of Fountainebleau*, 28; *Water Fantasy*, 28; *Who-o-s Who—The Great Horned Owl*, 92; *Wren's Gourd House*, 54

Mess, George Joseph: birth, 11; meets Evelynne Bernloehr, 9, 15; with family, moves to Indianapolis from Cincinnati, 12; contracts pneumonia and typhoid fever, 12; receives scholarship to Herron, 12; assists in construction of murals for City Hospital, 13; paints murals for the public grade school, 13; studies painting in night classes at Herron, 13; Works at Western Electric Company, 13; enlists in U. S. Army, 13; enrolls at Butler University, 15; founds Circle Art Company, 15; enrolls at Columbia University, 15; marriage, 17; with Evelynne, opens Circle Art Academy, 18; studies at Fontainebleau school, 19-20; resumes teaching at Circle Art Academy, 25; applies as student to Tiffany Foundation, 27; closes Circle Art Academy, 30; joins others in establishing Circle Engraving Company, 30; learns etching from Evelynne, 35; approach to printmaking, 35-36; acquires position with Esquire, Inc., 46; moves to Chicago, 46; works published in *Esquire*, 49; turns from etching to painting, 56; illness, 57, 59, 75-76; returns to Indianapolis, 57; with Evelynne, buys farm near Nashville (Indiana), 60; with Evelynne, sells share of engraving company, 60; illustrates Jeanette Covert Nolan's *Hoosier City, the Story of Indianapolis*, 60, 63; teaches at

Wayman Adams's school, 63-64; article published in *American Artist* about, 64; commissioned to create etching for Princeton Print Club, 64; teaches at downtown branch of Indiana University, 74, 75; teaches at Indianapolis Art League, 74; teaches at Herron, 74; death, 76; tributes at death, 76, 81; honored by programs, 85; becomes member of Indiana Society of Printmakers, 111

—awards received: for bookplate, 11; from Indianapolis Art Association, 27; at Indiana Artists' Club exhibits, 27, 64, 76; at State Fair, 30; at Hoosier Salon exhibits, 41, 59, 64, 76; at California Society of Etchers exhibit, 64; at Library of Congress exhibits, 64, 75; at Society of Etchers exhibits, 75; at Dallas National Print Competition, 75

—exhibits: Brown County Art Gallery, 93; Carnegie Institute, 27; Chicago Art Institute, 46; Chicago Century of Progress Exposition, 30; Cincinnati Art Museum, 27; Dayton Art Institute, 64; Herron Art Institute, 30, 32, 64, (memorial exhibit) 85, 112; Hoosier Salon, 19, 41, 49, 64, 76; Indiana Artists' Club, 59; Indianapolis Museum of Art (downtown gallery), 93, 99; Jewish Community Center, 76; June 1 Gallery (Connecticut), 93; Library of Congress, 64, 75; Lieber galleries, 64; Metropolitan Museum of Art, 75; National Academy of Design, 41, 64; Paris International Exhibition, 54; Pettis gallery, 20; Philadelphia Society of Etchers, 41; Seattle Art Museum, 41; Woman's Department Club, 25

—works mentioned: *Abode of the Boatmaker*, 46; *Across the Canal of Episy*, 20; *Adirondack Solitude*, 64; *Adirondacks*, 64; *After the Snow*, 13; *Around the Hilltop*, 59; *Aurora*, 41; *Backyard Romance*, 46; *The Barren Plum Tree*, 41; *Bayfield*, 54; *Brookside Bridge*, 27; *City of Rooftops*, 54; *Clouds of France*, 20; *Coastline*, 54; *Do Come Around*, 85; *Early Spring Patterns*, 76; *Ed Luckey's Farm*, 54; *Edge of the Forest*, 36, 41; *Ever So Humble*, 54, 59; *Fall Bouquet*, 76; *Foothills*, 76; *Full Moon*, 76; *Gardener's House*, 36; *The Goat Farm*, 64; *Highway No. 7*, 75; *Hill Top Pond*, 64; *The Hitching

Post, 60; *If Winter Comes*, 54; *In Full Moon*, 85; *In the Hills of Villecerf*, 20; *Indianapolis in Snow*, 27; *Lake Near Bean Blossom*, 76; *Living Better Without*, 64, 75; *Love*, 64; *Metamora*, 27, 36; *Neighbors*, 59; *Old Fairland Mill*, 54; *The Open Road*, 36; *Paradise Valley*, 76; *Plant Life in Moonlight*, 76; *Reelsfoot Bridge*, 54; *Sand Dune Cabins*, 54; *Sand Slopes*, 85; *Snow Covered City*, 85; *Southern France*, 20; *Southern Oak*, 85; *Summertime*, 36; *Tangled Branches*, 59; *Time for Rest*, 54; *Winter in Indianapolis*, 27, 54; *Winter in the Hills*, 59; *Winter Patterns*, 76; *Wishing Gate*, 54, 60; *Wishing Gate in Winter*, 59; *Wishing Well by Walk*, 76; *Work-shed*, 54

Mess, Gordon, 11, 15, 18, 19, 30, 60

Mess, Joseph J., 11, 12, 30

Metropolitan Museum of Art (N. Y.), 75

Metropolitan School of Music, 2

Miller, George, 112

Milliken, Mary B., Award for Excellence, 112

Modern Art Center (Brown County), 86

Morehouse, Lucille (quoted), 20, 25, 32, 74

Morlan, Dorothy, 13

National Academy of Design, 41, 63, 64

National League of American Penwomen, 93

National Oats Company, 11

National Society for Arts and Letters, 74, 75, 85

Nolan, Jeanette Covert, 63

Northwest Printmakers, 46

Ohio Society of Printmakers (Dayton), 60

Ouvré, Achile, 19, 20

Oxbow Acres, 86, 91

Palazzo, Tony, 54

Panama-Pacific International Exposition (San Francisco), 107

Peat, Wilbur David, 85, 108, 109, 110

Pennsylvania Academy of Fine Arts, 32, 109

Pettis gallery (Indianapolis), 20

Philadelphia Society of Etchers, 41

Philadelphia Society of Printmakers, 46

Phillips, Robert, 12

Colophon

This book is printed on 80-pound Dulcet Text of
the Monadnock Paper Mills, one of the finest
printing papers available at time of printing. Dulcet is a neutral white paper balanced and color-
corrected to reflect all the colors of the spectrum
uniformly without glare. It is a neutral ph archival
quality paper, a paper preferred by archivists and
conservators.

The Garamond typeface used throughout this
book is a 16th century classic designed by Claude
Garamond. One of the world's most widely used
typefaces in the first half of this century, it was
introduced in the American market in 1917 and
is still considered 'contemporary' by graphic
designers.

Book design by David Stahl (Herron Graduate)
Typography by Weimer Typesetting Company, Inc., Indianapolis
Printing by Benham Press, Inc., Indianapolis